SOLVE, NOT SERVE

SOLVE, NOT SERVE

WHAT OTHER NONPROFIT MANAGEMENT BOOKS WON'T TELL YOU

KELLY E. GRIFFIN

NEW DEGREE PRESS

COPYRIGHT © 2022 KELLY E. GRIFFIN

All rights reserved.

SOLVE, NOT SERVE

What Other Nonprofit Management Books Won't Tell You

ISBN	979-8-88504-112-6	*Paperback*
	979-8-88504-739-5	*Kindle Ebook*
	979-8-88504-218-5	*Ebook*

Contents

A Better Place?

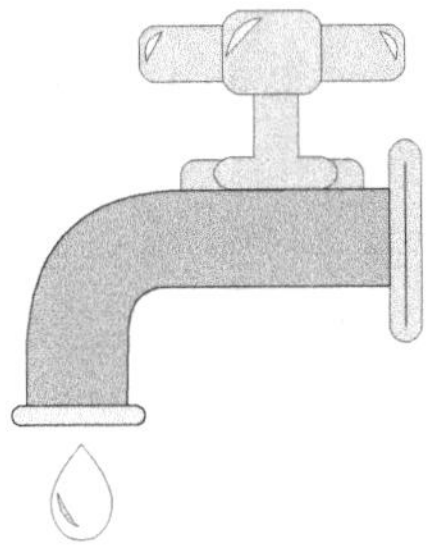

I began my do-gooding career right out of college at a behemoth nonprofit and never looked back. For many years, I was content that my work was helping people and—more grandly—making the world a better place. I didn't realize right away that many of the organizations I was toiling for were only having mediocre impacts on the state of the world.

What woke me up was my role at KABOOM!, the national nonprofit dedicated to play for children. Research shows that play is critical for healthy child development, including physical, cognitive, and social-emotional skills.

When I was hired to help create and implement a new organizational strategy in 2013, the organization had been building around two hundred playgrounds in low-income communities each year, serving a few thousand kids. However, even drastically scaling up our operations to build, say, two thousand playgrounds a year and serve tens of thousands more kids would still leave millions and millions behind and not solve the problem on the scale it exists. We also had to face the fact that even low-income kids living in the neighborhoods that KABOOM! served still had fewer opportunities to play because their families were less likely to have time to take them to the playground and other kid-friendly places.

We realized that we needed a different approach if we were going to impact the lives of more children. We changed our mission statement from "Giving every child in America a great place to play within walking distance," to "Ensuring that every kid, especially the sixteen million kids living in poverty, get the play they need to thrive.'

We first thought about where low-income kids were spending their time—often in adult spaces with their parents or caregivers running errands, waiting in line, and taking public transportation. This led us to consider how we could turn those spaces into play opportunities, so we began to think differently about infrastructure. We got creative about what would make a bus stop, grocery store, or laundromat more fun for kids.

It also led us to think about who influenced those spaces. We thought about who makes decisions about things like infrastructure, urban planning, and school policies, and we began to think differently about influence. We designed an "influence strategy" to influence decision makers (like municipal leaders and school system administrators) to create opportunities for kids to play more (like play infrastructure, keeping playgrounds open after hours, recess policies, etc.).

This different approach to both infrastructure and influence paved the way for us to not only reach more kids, but also reach them more meaningfully. If a low-income kid had a playful city bus stop in which to wait in the morning, recess at school, and a colorful hopscotch on the sidewalk along the way to the game-filled laundromat with mom after school, that kid was getting more opportunities to get the physical, cognitive, and social-emotional development benefits of play than if we had just built a playground near him.

This profound shift in KABOOM!'s strategy caused massive changes in nearly everything about the organization, from who we hired, with whom we partnered, and how we spoke about our work. Many of these changes were painful. Several funders did not support our new direction. Some staff felt displaced and angry. However, seeing that the changes were resulting in bigger and better impact made the hard parts easier. Every passionate, dedicated nonprofit employee should know this feeling!

This exposure taught me that strategic thinking can lead to real transformative impact. I also saw how difficult it was for an organization to drastically change how it operates. I wondered if other nonprofits were thinking this way or if they needed a bit of inspiration. So, I did some research on the history of nonprofits and how effective we are now, in 2022.

While we can trace the origins of the nonprofit sector to before the establishment of the American government, it was first recognized as a sector in the 1970s after the 1969 tax code created the 501(c)(3) designation. New nonprofits are founded every day; more than half a million nonprofits have been created in the last twenty years. As of 2020, there are 1.54 million nonprofits (Independent Sector 2022), accounting for 10 percent of the nation's workforce and more than 12.5 million employees, the third largest workforce of any US industry (Salamon and Newhouse, 2020). Most of these are relatively small organizations. More than 66 percent have annual budgets of less than five hundred thousand dollars (Urban Institute Brief 2020).

With very few exceptions, each of our over twelve million nonprofit employees believe they are making the world a better place. Nonprofit employees are among the most passionate, dedicated, selfless, hardworking people in the world. I have worked with and learned from some of the most amazing individuals and have been inspired by them every day. In addition, more than 25 percent of Americans—68 million people—volunteer their time and talent in nonprofits every year (Urban Institute Brief 2020).

Sadly, most of us are at least somewhat wrong about making the world a better place. Many inequities and other problems in our society are greater and more serious today than they were a few decades ago. Although the Great Recession of 2008 supposedly ended, the longitudinal Human Needs Index found that human needs in three quarters of US states were greater in 2017 than they were in 2007 (Human Needs Index 2018).

Even before the COVID-19 pandemic, we had a profoundly unstable and uncertain economy. Poverty rates are trending equal or greater to the Great Recession and haven't really improved much in fifty years (Census 2021). Economic mobility is stalled (Cowen, 2015). There continues to be increases in mental illness and substance abuse rates and deaths (World Health Organization 2022). Systemic racism and inequities in gender, sexuality, socioeconomic status, and age are still disadvantaging groups of people (Urban Institute Structural Racism 2020).

The pandemic exacerbated this dire situation, as rates of job instability and food and housing insecurity are trending even higher. The employment rate remains below pre-pandemic levels and millions of families are still behind on rent payments (although employment is rising and strains on household budgets have eased slightly since the darkest days of spring 2020). Due to our aforementioned systemic racism and inequity, the pandemic also had a disproportionately harsh impact on Black, Indigenous, and People of Color (BIPOC) and other marginalized groups in terms of access to health care, digital capability for remote work and school, and overrepresentation in high-risk "essential" jobs (CBPP 2021).

Recent studies find that most nonprofit organizations struggle to meet these needs. A database of over three thousand rigorously tested, evidence-based programs offers chilling information: Fewer than 37 percent of programs run by nonprofits have definite positive impacts. Only 50 percent of the programs had "promising evidence" of positive impacts, which doesn't inspire much confidence (Pew Results First 2015).

Unfortunately, this database and other similar ones only include the most sophisticated programs, so most of the nonprofit work we all do day-to-day does not even get evaluated. Even if we are comfortable extrapolating data from the most sophisticated programs to all programs, this means less than half of what we work so hard to do has meaningful, positive impacts on people's lives.

I am frustrated, because while nonprofit employees are making *some* things a *bit* better for *some* people, as a whole we are not really making much progress toward solving our worst social problems. As a nonprofit devotee, I want to do better! I want us *all* to do better!

I am compelled to dig into this topic because I have made a career of running toward big nonprofit changes like a firefighter runs toward a burning building. Over the last twenty years, I have helped more than a dozen nonprofits create and execute new strategies, working directly with CEOs and board leadership as both an internal staff person and an external consultant. I am also an executive coach, helping nonprofit leaders become more effective in their roles. Unfortunately, I have seen many organizations and leaders struggle with how to make the big changes in their organizations that would lead to real impact. As a result, many nonprofits continue to have only mediocre impact.

From my vantage point both inside and outside organizations, despite all our best intentions, I have seen a lot of what *not* to do. A lot of making timid, incremental steps. A lot of hemorrhaging time, talent, and treasure on minimally useful activities. A lot of avoiding risk and covering your ass. A lot of how not to be effective.

I am also compelled to share what I have learned from my experiences and observations, because it seems like many nonprofit management books and articles suggest for-profit business management principles only slightly revised for nonprofits. Thanks to the inimitable Vu Le, former nonprofit executive and brilliant writer behind the *Nonprofit AF* blog, I now think of that as "bizsplaining." Frankly, I find bizsplaining really annoying. Since the missions, the impacts, and the funding mechanisms of nonprofits are fundamentally different from (the vast majority of) for-profit businesses, why do so many of these authors believe both should operate the same way? I solemnly swear that I will not bizsplain anything to you.

I've been in the trenches and have seen firsthand the failure of some of the stuff they tell us in those books and articles. I also interviewed dozens of awe-inspiring changemakers who didn't follow the traditional advice and are making—or well on their way to making—massive impact. I am here to challenge some of what those bizsplainy books and articles say and share what really works!

If nonprofit organizations want to make real impact on social problems—and those of us who work there want to know we're making the world a better place—we need to go much bigger and bolder. Massive problems are only going to be solved by massive actions. The vast majority of nonprofits are not set up to take massive actions, so the organizations need to make major internal changes to set them up for success.

This is not just "outside-the-box" thinking. This is "set the box on fire, throw it over a cliff, and start inventing entirely new shapes" thinking. Nonprofits need to abandon tentative, safe changes that serve people. They need to adopt radical, transformational, tectonic-plate shifting changes to *solve* problems like poverty, hunger, homelessness, racism, abuse, and discrimination—or at the very least, get closer to solving them.

Unfortunately, many of us in the nonprofit sector don't know how to make these changes. A variety of factors make this kind of bold confidence elusive. Taking risks is hard and scary. We understandably worry about what funders and donors will think and do. We worry about failing and being punished for those failures with shame, ridicule, and career-harming retributions. I want all nonprofit leaders (current and future—leadership can come from anywhere) to find the conviction, grasp the knowledge, and take the big risks necessary for big gains.

This book is for you if you work in, volunteer for, or fund a nonprofit and want to stop being frustrated all the time; if you want to be part of truly meaningful, transformative change in our world. This book will challenge some traditional thinking and motivate you with stories of true impact—on individuals and on our society. This book will inspire you to lead from wherever you sit.

Wouldn't it be awesome to say you helped eradicate polio and saved millions of people from severe illness and death, or that you played a part in creating a TV show that resulted in early-childhood learning gains for millions of kids, or that you contributed to providing 96 percent of Americans with easy access to free libraries? There are people out there who can say those things, largely because they contributed to the kinds of organizations that did some of the very same things I highlight in this book. They concentrated on real impact, not outputs and scattershot programming. They built the right kind of leaders with effective structures around them. They identified and leaned into brave decisions. They recognized what is unique about our sector and only borrowed what was helpful from the for-profit sector. Lastly, they navigated the funding landscape with savvy and aplomb.

What social problems will the next generation solve? Could you help eradicate homelessness? Could you play a role in ending over four hundred years of systemic racism? Could you be a part of curing cancer and saving millions of lives? All Americans should want the nonprofit sector to succeed. However, it is those of us who work in, volunteer for, and fund these organizations that have the real power.

I once saw a political cartoon that I often think of in relation to nonprofit work (even though it was about another topic). It's a depiction of two people mopping the floor while beside them a faucet is on full blast. C'mon, my fellow nonprofit people, let's turn off the damn faucet. Let's *Solve, Not Serve*!

PART 1

HISTORY HAS ITS EYES ON YOU

The American nonprofit sector has been around for centuries. However, never in our country's history have our problems and challenges felt more astounding and intractable. Never has the need felt this obvious across so many issues at once—poverty, public health, systemic racism, immigration, and others.

Consequently, never in our history has the nonprofit sector had a greater opportunity to rip these social problems out at the roots. This country has never before had more attention on our problems, more accumulated wealth, and more ability to communicate with and organize its people.

Now is the time to fight our huge social problems. Now is the time to *solve* these problems. In Part 1, we will explore the potential of the nonprofit sector and why now is the perfect time for our sector to rise to the occasion.

CHAPTER 1.1

Why Us

"Nonprofit organizations provide many of the most distinctive features of life in the United States. It is through self-governing nonprofit organizations that Americans have expressed—and managed—their religious, cultural, and ethnic diversity..."
—DAVID HAMMACK, AUTHOR AND PROFESSOR OF HISTORY EMERITUS AT CASE WESTERN RESERVE UNIVERSITY

THE BIRTH OF THE US NONPROFIT SECTOR

In the United States, the origins of the nonprofit sector predate the formation of our government. The early settlers formed charitable and mutual aid networks like hospitals, fire departments, and orphanages to help their neighbors and confront social issues.

After the American Revolution, once we had our new government and a dominant middle class, we developed a limited welfare state where our government committed to protect the health and well-being of its citizens (Arnsberger et al, 2008). Some of our foundational American political beliefs, such as the limited role of government in general, low taxes, and the separation of church and state, provided fertile ground for charitable organizations. As a young country, we decided to establish charitable organizations to fill the gaps in government social welfare programs. It has also been posited that early Americans embraced charitable organizations over government programs because they feared monarchy or bureaucracy (Arnsberger et al, 2008).

In the early twentieth century, a number of American industrialists like Cornelius Vanderbilt, Andrew Carnegie, and John D. Rockefeller created private foundations to direct their wealth to altruistic pursuits. These industrialists thought it was their duty to alleviate the suffering of those less fortunate. Generally speaking, only white males were able to amass wealth at that time.

After the Civil War ended, charitable institutions grew to include those that helped Black people and other disadvantaged groups. For example, Reconstruction inspired people like banker George Peabody and philanthropist John F. Slater to establish early philanthropic foundations to support education in the South (Black Education 2000).

Nonprofit organizations grew slowly but steadily between 1900 and 1960. Some legal and administrative rules and practices, such as simple procedures for creating a nonprofit, promoted the growth of the number of organizations. However, there were also significant restrictions on growth. Black people, women, and "dissidents" often encountered resistance when seeking nonprofit charters (Hammack, 2001).

CIVIL RIGHTS AND NONPROFIT GROWTH

Nonprofits saw remarkable growth in the 1960s for three major reasons: increasing American wealth, the Civil Rights movement, and the expansion of government caused by both that movement and the Great Society programs of President Lyndon B. Johnson (Hammack, 2001).

In this era, Americans had more money to spend. Average per capita incomes more than doubled from 1945 to 1990, and Americans quadrupled their spending on all services—including those provided by nonprofits—in the same timeframe. However, it was not just this increase in demand for services that tripled the nonprofit sector's share of the American economy (Hammack, 2001).

According to nonprofit historian David Hammack, the Civil Rights movement led to new ideas about the role of both the government and nonprofit organizations. While our country was still divided on individual rights, liberal entities like labor unions and lawmakers in the North would not support federal funding of things like health or education because of the inequitable way it may have been implemented in the South. The passage of the Civil Rights Act in 1964 paved the way for Congress' approval of federal funding for health care, education, and social services.

The Civil Rights movement also resulted in federal courts removing the previous barriers that Black people and women had encountered when they tried to start nonprofit organizations (Hammack, 2001).

Also, the Great Society programs of the 1960s—like Medicaid and Medicare—boosted the nonprofit sector because they sharply increased subsidies and paid for services that may be provided by private as well as government agencies. Many Great Society programs provided funds directly to nonprofits. For example, federal funding went directly to Head Start programs for preschool children as part of education reform (Hammack, 2001).

The nonprofit sector was first recognized as an actual sector in 1970s due to the 1969 tax code. There are five qualifications for an organization to qualify for tax exemption under section 501(c)(3): have some organizational structure, do not distribute profits, do not devote substantial amount of resources to lobbying, do not engage in partisan political activity, and be engaged in several specified exempt activities. Exempt activities include those that are charitable, religious, educational, scientific, literary, testing for public safety, and preventing cruelty to children or animals (Internal Revenue Service 2022).

Despite their name, nonprofits also report net income (the difference between revenue and expenses) to the IRS. They use information about their financial status to attract additional funding, make investments, and justify expansion (Arnsberger et al, 2008).

After the tax designation, the "new" nonprofit sector exploded. Nonprofit expenditures as a share of US wages increased by 36 percent in the 1970s and then doubled between 1980 and the mid-1990s. During this time, our federal government began to rely even more heavily on nonprofit organizations to distribute goods and services (Hammack, 2001).

OUR SECTOR TODAY

The US nonprofit sector is the largest in the world with over $1.7 trillion in total revenue in 2016. New nonprofits are started every day. As of 2020, there are 1.54 million nonprofits. There are 12.5 million nonprofit employees (Salamon and Newhouse, 2020), more than 64 million nonprofit board members and volunteers, and tens of millions of donors (Independent Sector 2022). The nonprofit sector's payroll exceeds that of most other US industries, including construction, transportation, manufacturing, and finance, and trails behind only retail and food service (Salamon and Newhouse, 2020).

American nonprofit organizations continue to fulfill critical capacities that government cannot. For example, nonprofits provide about 70 percent of community hospital care and educate about 30 percent of students enrolled in four-year colleges (Meehan and Jonker, 2019). Our nonprofit sector is an important delivery system for government-funded social services, including but not limited to health care, education, transportation, police, fire service, job training, subsidized housing, mental health services, elder care, childcare, foster care, and food subsidies.

Nonprofit organizations also play significant roles in shaping our society. Nonprofit research universities set national models and standards in scientific research. Education nonprofits create curricula, standardized testing for students, and accreditation of teachers. Other nonprofit organizations set national standards in fields like engineering and health care. Nonprofit organizations provide much of our nation's cultural and performing arts, including museums and theaters. "It is through self-governing nonprofits… that Americans have developed the competitive variety of their hospitals, research universities and liberal arts colleges, research institutes, think tanks, and cultural and arts organizations," wrote Hammack (Hammack 2002).

Most of the time, nonprofits are working to solve things that government and the marketplace can't (or won't) solve. We are the only sector that can combine government, corporate, and philanthropic funding, which equates to a lot of power.

However, we are not meeting the chilling amount of need in America. As we covered in the introduction, our poverty rates, lack of economic mobility, housing and food insecurity, mental health challenges, and racism and inequity are all still massive problems. This need is overwhelming our sector. The Nonprofit Finance Fund's 2018 survey assessing the state of the nonprofit sector produced some sobering data. A full 86 percent of nonprofits surveyed reported the demand for their services was rising, yet 57 percent reported that they cannot meet the demand.

In *Engine of Impact*, authors William F. Meehan III and Kim Starkey Jonker characterize the American nonprofit sector as the "impoverished stepchild of business and government. It remains chronically underfunded, relies extensively on voluntary gifts of time and money… and delivers services that benefit society overall but whose natural supporters are disparate and unorganized."

Beginning in 2020, the pandemic had a pronounced impact on nonprofits of all sizes. Forty percent reported losses in total revenue for 2020, and those 40 percent lost an average of 31 percent of total revenue and 7 percent of paid staff. The pandemic-related curtailment in nonprofit services also caused a dramatic decline in program-related income. These factors exacerbated the financial challenges of many nonprofit organizations and our sector as a whole (Faulk et al, 2021).

In our perpetually underfunded and resource-stretched state, the only option we have is to get better, get more strategic, and get more effective at solving big problems.

But why now? What's the urgency?

Why Now

———

A perfect storm is currently upon us in the nonprofit sector. External forces are colliding with internal tensions and creating colossal opportunity—opportunity for individual organizations and the sector as a whole to move from serving people affected by intractable social problems to actually solving those intractable problems.

Engine of Impact authors Meehan and Jonker say we are at the dawn of a new nonprofit era called "The Impact Era," in which nonprofits will play an even more vital role in supporting, safeguarding, and sustaining American civil society. According to them, "All of us—nonprofit executives, philanthropists, grant makers, board members, and everyday donors and citizens—must answer a question that is fundamental to our collective future: do we want a robust, high-performing nonprofit sector, or don't we? If the answer is yes, then we must move forward boldly."

I fully agree with these authors on this point. As we discussed in the last chapter, Americans have collectively placed a lot of responsibility on the nonprofit sector. American need is escalating, and the stakes are higher now than ever before.

Many of us in the sector are recognizing that everything about what we do—our missions, our culture, our operating structures—needs to evolve rapidly. Why? Let's talk about some macro trends.

PACE OF SOCIAL CHANGE

Many studies show rapid and accelerating rates of social change in the last one hundred years. When defining social change, researchers from both sociology and psychology distinguish two types based on the pace of change: incremental and dramatic. The accelerating pace that we currently feel is due to more rapidly evolving incremental changes (where elements of a system are continually adjusting as conditions change) as well as more instances of dramatic changes (where there is a complete break from the past) (Pestana and Codina, 2019).

This increasing pace is due to various factors, including scientific and technological inventions and our super abundance of everything from capital to talent. We now live in an exponential world. For example, it took twenty-two years for fifty million people to begin using televisions, fourteen years for fifty million people to begin using computers, seven years for fifty million people to begin using the internet, and nineteen *days* for fifty million people to begin playing Pokémon GO (Desjardins, 2018).

Adam Fong, program officer in the Hewlett Foundation's Performing Arts program, encountered this increasing pace in his work with grantees it funds in the San Francisco Bay Area arts community. "Our previous strategy, which focused on sustaining exemplary organizations, was not keeping up with what was relevant. We shifted our strategy in the last couple of years because the changes in the world were moving so much faster than these nonprofits were able to evolve; we needed to seek new grantees that are representative of rapidly evolving demographics and culture."

GOVERNMENT AND OTHER CENTRALIZED SYSTEMS

This accelerating pace of social change is taking its toll on our government and related systems. Over the last decade-ish, we have seen various systems being broken and reinvented, as trust in institutions steadily declines. James Siegal, former CEO of KABOOM! and one of my favorite trend watchers, provided a great example: "Financial systems are being reinvented right now. Someone who's looking to have access to what banks typically offer has so many more options. Many young people are not opening up a bank account but have a Robin Hood account [a fee-free platform to trade in the stock market] or even a cryptocurrency wallet. That goes for those who are dissatisfied with the major financial institutions and also for those who have been excluded from the mainstream financial system, providing new opportunities for what some people describe as the 'unbanked,'" he said.

This trend of democratizing finance is forcing systems to adjust. "If you take a step back and line that up with trends like giving directly to the people who need the money, and all the experiments that are happening around providing basic income, these things are suggesting that our financial systems are being completely disrupted," Siegal concluded.

Our government systems are also feeling pressure from this growing dissatisfaction with—and distrust in—institutions and a societal trend toward more libertarian values. While only 11 percent of Americans self-identify as Libertarian with a capital "L" (the belief that society should maximize individual freedom by minimizing governmental enforcement of economic, personal, and social concerns), a significantly higher percentage trend toward a blend of social liberal permissiveness and fiscal conservatism (Silver, 2015).

This means many people want a smaller role for government and are trying to push government out of certain issues. These massive systems changes indicate that many of the things that create the very need for nonprofits are in flux.

RACIAL JUSTICE

Another major trend is the awakening around racial justice that has happened over the last few years. Many Americans are now more acutely aware of systemic racism—the fact that we have structures and systems that are designed to continue to oppress certain people and communities. Racism played an active role in the creation of our education, health care, land ownership, criminal justice, and employment systems, and those biases persist today (Systemic Equality 2022).

This means that no matter what the social problem is—from disease to homelessness to the justice system—the situation is worse for BIPOC due to hundreds of years of systemic racism. A BIPOC individual with disease X is less likely to have access to the best health care, as well as more likely to have their symptoms dismissed by medical professionals (Agrawal and Enekwechi, 2020). A BIPOC who is homeless is more likely to be impacted by barriers to wealth accumulation and home ownership. A BIPOC in the justice system is more likely to be there due to bias or racial profiling, more likely to have been falsely accused, and more likely to have been given the maximum sentence. Many of these social problems are also disproportionately experienced by other marginalized groups, including ethnic minorities, LGBTQA individuals, religious groups, etc.

INTERSECTION OF GOVERNMENT SYSTEMS CHANGE AND RACIAL JUSTICE

A meaningful intersection exists between the growing push to decentralize power and the moral imperative to dismantle systemic racism. A lot of Americans are questioning who has the power to decide on how our society is structured and regulated. Many of our nonprofit organizations were started *for* people and communities but not *with* people and communities. There is a currently expanding belief that only the people and communities themselves have the power to make decisions for themselves about what they need and want.

This trend toward decentralized power is putting pressure on both government and the nonprofit sector. Both need to figure out how to share or transfer decision making to people who are members of the community. Different forms of organization are emerging. For example, according to the nonprofit legal center Sustainable Economies Law Center, a worker self-directed nonprofit is a cross between a worker cooperative with a 501(c)(3) nonprofit. In this structure, all workers have the power to influence the organization's programs, workplace conditions, and the direction of the organization as a whole—a true democratization of the traditional organizational structure.

Social justice and equity are also a driving force behind systems disruption, like in the financial systems example above. If banking and other financial services had always been accessible to low-income, low-wealth, and other disadvantaged people and communities, we would have no need to disrupt it to make it so.

PRESSURE FROM THE FOR-PROFIT SECTOR

The for-profit sector has recently made some very public gains in creating positive social good. Think of Wegman's cutting out tobacco products, or Patagonia pulling all business from Jackson Hole Mountain Resort after the owner held a fundraiser for a cause that did not align with their corporate values. John Kern of Beta Strategy Group (and former principal at Community Wealth Partners) said, "You have a majority of retail workers that are now paid fifteen dollars an hour, and while that was partly influenced by the social sector's longstanding push for a living wage and examples set in some progressive cities, the real tipping point was in response to pandemic-fueled changes in the economy and labor market. Retailers that had long ignored the push from social movements acted based on the stark economic realization that they must treat employees better in order to survive and grow."

In some cases, these companies are moving more rapidly on creating positive social good than organizations in our sector, which is designed to create positive good. Are we comfortable with the for-profit sector outpacing us on this? Personally, it gives me pause.

When it comes down to it, for-profits are focused on profit. Once the public recognition, employee loyalty, and sales growth winds down, they can drop social good programs and go back to business as usual. Their long-term focus remains their bottom line. I put much more trust in an organization with a mission to improve poverty or reduce hunger to do those things than a company that sells socks or ice cream.

This is not to say that the for-profit sector does not have an important role to play in helping us solve our big societal problems. They can push us, partner with us, and support us in our missions. Some for-profits actually include social missions in their charters. But those of us with the missions should be the ones in the lead.

All these macro trends add up to urgency. How can we use this perfect storm of need and opportunity to get down to the business of solving big problems?

PART 2

BRACE YOURSELF FOR IMPACT

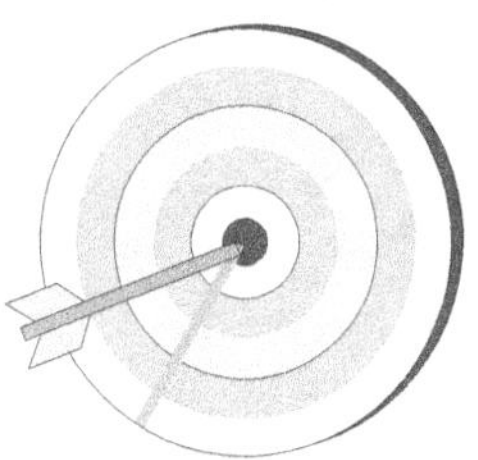

Other books say grow your *numbers*; I say grow your *impact*.

Most nonprofits have programs that help people. Many organizations have an assortment of programs; some programs serve people in smaller ways, some serve people in bigger ways, and some do everything in between.

As nonprofit leaders, we are always making difficult decisions about how to spend our resources, including human, financial, and social capital. We are often beholden to funders who expect us to report numbers and also expect these numbers to grow over time.

I propose that we focus on solving and not serving. Let us focus on true impact, not just numbers. Are we helping a person today, helping that person for years to come, or are we solving the problem that led her to need help in the first place?

In Part 2, we will examine what it means to go upstream to where the real solutions to problems live. We will discuss how to find a laser focus on where you're going and what sacrifices that may entail along the way. We will learn how to ensure you are making progress on getting to true impact.

Go Upstream

Why should we want to solve and not just serve? In his pivotal book *Upstream*, bestselling author Dan Heath says, "The reason to house the homeless or prevent disease or feed the hungry is not because of the financial returns, but because of the moral returns." I agree. Serving someone today and making their life better, easier, and less unfair is powerful. However, to solve the problem that led them to need help is even more powerful. It is how we can truly make the world a better place. To do this we need to focus on true impact.

What is impact? Briefly, I think we all know the difference between outputs (things you do or create) and outcomes (effects of those outputs on the people you help). The difference between outcomes and impacts is less well understood. Impacts go a step further than outcomes. An impact is a significant, longer-term change or benefit to a community or society. Ideally, an impact is directly attributable to the work of your organization. A simple example is if you eat healthy food and count calories (outputs), your outcome may be to lose ten pounds, but the impact will be a healthier body overall (you're putting less stress on your joints, you may be sleeping better, your cholesterol may be lower, etc.) as a result of your new healthy habits.

As you might imagine, impacts are the hardest to measure. We'll cover much more on that in a few chapters. Right now, we're going to discuss what impacts we should be striving for, and why.

SCARCE RESOURCES

As nonprofit leaders, deciding how to spend our human, financial, and other resources is one of our most challenging responsibilities. Because a lot of the advice we are given is to be more like for-profit businesses (more on that in Part 5), we often focus on return on investment, better known as ROI or "bang for our buck." A newer concept called "Social Return on Investment" monetizes the costs avoided or benefits gained from nonprofit work.

Many of our funders push us to report numbers that grow over time, heedless of the actual outcomes or impacts of our work (much more on that in Part 6). Funders are often fluent in the language of business and want to see our work reflected in numbers and budgets. However, nonprofit work is more about outcomes and impacts on actual people, and those intangibles are difficult to capture in terms of costs and spending.

Another challenge we have in our world of scarce resources is that we want to be able to help as many people as possible. I have seen so many nonprofits with portfolios of programs that have ballooned over time. Because each program was conceived to help people—real people whose names and stories we know—we typically have trouble making the decision to cut programs. This is true even if we know these programs are serving only a few people, only serving them in small ways, or not generating a good ROI. We struggle with who we may no longer help in that particular way with that particular program, and our nonprofit hearts feel like they're breaking.

You may have heard the parable about the babies in the river. To summarize, two people notice babies floating down the river. One jumps in and starts frantically pulling the babies out of the river, while the other runs upstream to stop whatever is putting the babies in the river in the first place. Hence, the terms "upstream" and "downstream." Upstream is where you find the root cause of a problem.

To help people in profound ways, when given the choice of where to invest our precious, scarce resources, our answer must be as proactive and as far upstream as possible. Uncomfortably, we spend so much energy and resources on reactive downstream programs that we collectively haven't gathered enough evidence to know where the right point in the stream is to solve many major problems (Heath, 2020).

Nonprofits have mostly confined ourselves to one tiny part of the stream: respond and react. For example, we spend billions to recover from hurricanes and earthquakes while chronically underfunding disaster preparedness. Don't even get me started on the costs (human and financial) of dealing with a raging pandemic versus public health efforts around pandemic prevention. Will we get it right next time?

THE SIREN CALL OF DOWNSTREAM

Much like a personal health issue, the symptoms of a needed social change are what alerts you to the problem. For example, you see homeless people sleeping in the streets or kids coming to school without having eaten breakfast. However, you can get stuck treating just the symptom. When you have a headache, solving that downstream symptom by reaching for the aspirin bottle is tempting because it requires a lot more time and energy to consider the reason for your headache. Determining that your headache is caused by an upstream reason like caffeine withdrawal, eye strain, or sleep deprivation takes a lot more brain power, and the solutions (more coffee, less screen time, better sleep) may not be as immediate or convenient as just swallowing a pill.

Similarly, downstream symptoms of societal problems are much more tangible. These symptoms are easier to identify and fix. We can give people blankets. We can feed them. It is easy to see and measure how these activities help people and restore them to their original state. Restoration, seeing people warm and fed, is heartening.

According to Dan Heath, there are three main reasons we—as humans and as nonprofit leaders—get stuck in downstream thinking:

- Problem blindness: "I don't see the problem." The belief that negative outcomes are natural or inevitable.
- Lack of ownership: "That problem is not mine to fix." When everyone believes the problem is not theirs to solve, or that the responsibility of the problem belongs to someone else.

- Tunneling: "I can't deal with that right now." The feeling of being overwhelmed and unable to prioritize. Tunneling comes from scarcity, whether that's of time, resources, or even mental bandwidth. Scarcity reduces our cognitive capacity and makes us less insightful, less forward-thinking, and less controlled. In the tunnel, there is only one narrow way forward and only room for short-term, reactive thinking (Heath, 2020).

While all three of these reasons are prevalent, the one I see as our biggest barrier to moving more upstream as a sector is tunneling. Tunneling is the reason for those ballooning portfolios of programs and haphazard decision making about resources. When you are tunneling, you cannot engage in proactivity, big-picture, long-term thinking, or make the best decisions about how to use scarce resources.

I am sure most of us did some tunneling during the COVID-19 pandemic. Personally, there was a time early on when I felt so overwhelmed by all the horrible news, the burden of remote work, and my inability to leave the house that I played one ridiculous, mindless game on my phone every night until 4:00 a.m. Was this good for my mental or physical health? Certainly not, but I could not see outside of the tunnel. I could not prioritize what was most important (like paid work, exercise, and sleep). I could not make better choices. I could not see the bigger picture. The game was my tunnel.

Relevant to much of our work in nonprofits, being poor often leads to tunneling. The experience of poverty reduces a person's bandwidth, and the lack of resources is one of the most intractable scarcities to resolve. Researchers have found that when a person experiences scarcity of money or time or mental bandwidth, little problems crowd out the big ones (Heath, 2020). You do not prioritize the biggest issues, you play Whac-A-Mole with less consequential ones. Do you ever look at your looming to-do list and pick the easiest item first? I've been known to put off doing work projects for gems like "take out garbage" or "find blue scarf." Imagine if those to-do list items were "find job," "pay rent," and "get car repaired."

To make matters worse, being reactive can be emotionally rewarding. As Heath says, "There's a kind of glory that comes from stopping a big screw-up at the last second. Look at all the clichés we have at our disposal… putting out the fire, saving the day, bailing us out… Saving the day feels awfully good and heroism is addictive."

Unfortunately, reactive downstream interventions are often not permanent or even semi-permanent fixes. Focusing on downstream programs can exhaust your resources and pull your focus from addressing the source of the symptoms. We cannot let that happen. We need to keep asking ourselves, "Is this the symptom of something else?" and keep pushing upstream.

BENEFITS OF UPSTREAM

"Part of *every* [nonprofit] organization's mission should be to push upstream. To prevent wounds as well as bandage them; to eliminate injustices as well as assisting those who suffered them," says Dan Heath.

An upstream solution—one that addresses a problem at its source—is broader, slower, and hazier than solving that problem downstream. Share Our Strength cofounder Billy Shore says, "Feeding a child is easy; solving poverty is hard." The sources of downstream symptoms can be complex. The downstream symptom is child hunger, and the upstream source is poverty, but how does one fix poverty?

One symptom sometimes has multiple sources. Other times, a symptom will be several steps downstream from the ultimate source. For example, poverty is caused by poor education, inadequate access to opportunity, and lack of social services, just for starters. Going upstream on poverty is therefore very complicated.

Going upstream is also frustratingly ambiguous because sometimes the measurement is actually what *doesn't* happen. Public health is the classic example of upstream work. Preventive public health efforts succeed when nothing happens. In the year 1900, one in five children did not live to see their fifth birthday. Today, fewer than one in five thousand children die before age five (CDC, 2022). Why? Because of upstream public health initiatives like better hygiene, cleaner water, and pasteurization, as well as sewage systems, antibiotics, and vaccines (Heath, 2020). You can imagine how many years or even decades it took to show results from those initiatives—that fewer young children were dying.

Unfortunately, this measuring-what-doesn't-happen situation makes upstream work feel more optional than downstream interventions. Bringing attention to upstream work is much harder because it can feel so hypothetical. If it works, it is often thankless. When you are downstream, the rescues, responses, and reactions are clear and present. The hurricane hits, the levees break, and what we need to do to save lives is clear. Predicting the levees can be breached and proactively shoring them up before the next big storm gets far less attention.

As you can see from these examples, going upstream generally involves systems change; you force the system to change, or at least make changes within the system. A well-designed system is the best upstream intervention. Systems change can take many years, like the tobacco wars or reducing our use of the chlorofluorocarbons that destroy the ozone layer.

Clearly, you need patience and stubbornness when you go upstream if you are going to weather the uncertain time horizons, skeptics, and lack of tangible results. You also need courage and a fair measure of humility. However, the goal of upstream work is to eliminate the need for patience, stubbornness, courage, and humility and actually put ourselves out of business.

SWIMMING UPSTREAM

I am not suggesting that we abandon downstream work. We don't want to stop rescuing people and reacting to the problems we see. There's an old adage about an ounce of prevention being worth a pound of cure. We are currently providing billions of pounds of downstream cures, but I agree with Heath: We are capable of greater things.

He offers three suggestions for pushing upstream:

1) Be impatient for action but patient for outcomes and impacts.

Since solving problems further upstream can take decades, you need to celebrate each small victory along the journey. This will mean identifying the right short-term and longer-term outcomes on your way to impacts. (I'll stop here for now because we are going to go deep on measurement in Chapter 2.3.)

2) Macro starts with micro.

You cannot help many people until you understand how to help one. You cannot understand a problem until you've seen it up close—gotten proximate. This is something familiar to me from my two degrees in anthropology. In anthropology we often use a technique called the ethnographic method. The crux of the ethnographic method is participant observation, which is open-ended, inductive, full immersion in a "culture" to gain understanding of local knowledge, values, and practices from the "native's" point of view. It results in a vast amount of qualitative data.

The ethnographic method is very useful in better understanding problems. For example, anthropologists in San Francisco joined a multidisciplinary team to determine why mammogram rates were lower in Latina women. Health disparities expert and lead researcher Rena Pasick, DrPH, felt the ethnographic approach was a game changer. "I've worked in very diverse communities over the past twenty years and just couldn't find research tools that adequately explained the behavior I was seeing… Anthropology and the social sciences opened up entire new ways of understanding," she said. The team planned to use their findings to develop more effective methods of encouraging Latina women to get mammograms (Hindery, 2009).

However, even nonprofits without in-house anthropologists can seek better understanding of the problems they wish to solve. Share Our Strength's No Kid Hungry campaign regularly invites chefs and other influencers to join impact trips where they can see kids happily eating school breakfasts and lunches and speak with the school personnel who are responsible for the kids' learning. This opportunity to observe the work in action often moves these individuals to get involved in fighting child hunger.

3) Favor scoreboards over pills.

Sometimes nonprofit leaders think we need to approach developing a successful program like a pharmaceutical company develops a new drug. We think we need to get it absolutely perfect before we go to scale. We let the perfect become the enemy of the good. Dan Heath contrasts the pill model with a mindset focused on continuous improvement—what he calls the scoreboard model. This is where you begin with something good but are not afraid to scale and learn at the same time. Keep tweaking your program, asking "How can we make progress this week?"

When it comes to striving for real upstream solutions, even a defeat is effectively a victory because each defeat teaches us something. (We'll cover this in depth in Part 4.)

Now, to monitor and measure your progress on that journey—to know what to put on the scoreboard—is a whole other kettle of fish that we will talk about in the next chapter.

Laser Focus

No matter where in the stream you focus your efforts, the operative term here is "focus." Without focus, your organization will likely generate outputs and maybe even some outcomes, but you cannot expect impacts. *Engine of Impact* authors Meehan and Jonker have some strong words about this: "Breadth of mission, often accompanied by vagueness, is a prevalent virus in the nonprofit sector and the cause of its most severe chronic disease, commonly known as mission creep. Nonprofits routinely extend themselves… far beyond their core competencies."

Researchers who analyzed panel data involving nonprofits over a five-year period in the *Journal of Management* found that the main relationship between program diversification and efficiency is an inverted U shape. Basically, nonprofits that added new programs experienced some initial efficiencies, but then very quickly became more inefficient (Meehan and Jonker, 2019).

Having a laser focus on a narrow set of programs is especially critical when you consider that most nonprofits are small and limited in resources and capacity. Even big nonprofits are unlikely to have the resources and capacity to support successful execution of more than a very limited number of programs. Unfortunately, nonprofits have been trending toward increasing their number of activities in the final decades of the twentieth century through today (Meehan and Jonker, 2019).

Many experts—myself included—feel that poor quality of strategic planning and implementation is hampering non-profits' ability to focus, therefore preventing them from achieving stability in their operations, accomplishing their missions, and solving big social problems.

SO HOW DO YOU GET FOCUS?

The backbone of a nonprofit organization is its mission (the "what"). A great mission statement is clear, focused, and fully aligned with the organization's capabilities. Many organizations have pretty clear mission statements, but frequently things get ambiguous after that. How do you get from your lofty mission statement to the design and execution of specific activities and programs—your actual work? I recommend creating a theory of change and a strategic plan.

A theory of change (ToC) is a testable hypothesis of how your organization causes change and achieves its mission. It presents a causal pathway—essentially the "why" and also the "how" of what you do. It is a really clear, visual way to show stakeholders like potential funders, partners, and even new staff and board members how your organization makes an impact.

If ToCs are so great, why doesn't every nonprofit organization have one? To be perfectly honest, I don't know. Some organizations have logic models instead, which do serve a purpose, but they are generally less useful than ToCs because they do not include the "why." The Nonprofit Finance Fund's 2018 survey revealed that 53 percent of nonprofits do not have a ToC *or* a logic model. Some organizations just have strategic plans. Every organization should absolutely have a strategic plan—more on that later—but you should also have a clear ToC.

Sample Theory of Change

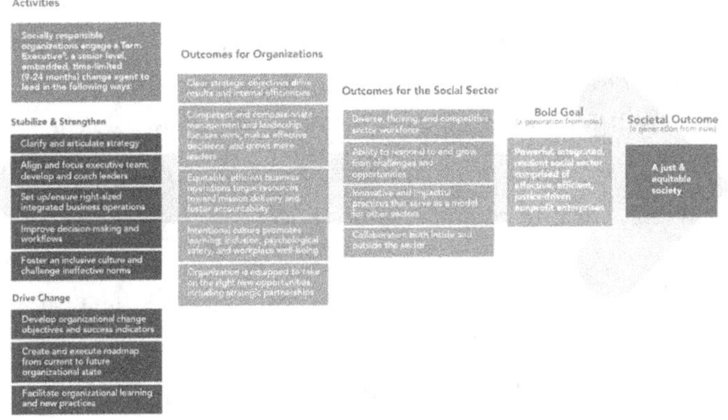

Briefly, a ToC is built from right to left. You start all the way to the right with what big societal outcome is the ultimate "why" of your organization. This societal outcome you are striving for should be a generation from now and really aspirational. For example, if you are a local food bank, your ultimate societal outcome might be to end hunger in your county. If you are a national health organization, your ultimate outcome might be to cure disease X.

The next step in building your ToC is to move left on the diagram and define your Bold Goal. This Bold Goal should also be a generation from now, or at least fifteen to twenty years. If the ultimate societal outcome is the pie, the Bold Goal is your organization's slice. This is what your organization is holding itself accountable for, so it should be clear, achievable, and, well… bold. It should inspire your staff, stakeholders, and potential partners.

Moving left on the diagram again, you should consider your outcomes next. Your outcomes are the changes you seek to create that will add up to your Bold Goal. These outcomes need to be true in order for you to achieve your Bold Goal. Having different outcomes for different audiences—such as the general public, policymakers, businesses, or a particular field (e.g. law enforcement)—is common for organizations.

All the way to the left on the diagram, you indicate your current activities. The fun part will be adding the causal pathways (usually arrows) that indicate which activities lead to which outcomes. There are often surprises here! For example, one time when I was leading ToC creation with a client, the CEO had an "aha!" moment when she realized the scientific reports the organization produced were not intended to convince the public of anything. They were not even intended to be read by lay people; they were specifically intended to build the organization's credibility within the scientific community. This caused her to better understand how the science department should fit into the overall structure of the organization.

You also may discover that you have an outcome that does not have enough activities with causal pathways to it. If that outcome is truly critical for the achievement of your Bold Goal, you may need to add activities to ensure it happens. On the flip side—the side that is often so difficult for nonprofits—you may discover an activity that does not link to any of your outcomes. It may be time to sunset that activity, which will feel sad but will actually free up resources for activities that do clearly lead to outcomes.

I have helped many nonprofits develop their ToCs. As awesome as it is to have the finished diagram so that your stakeholders better understand your organization, the process of creating a ToC is just as important as the product. Collaboratively building your ToC creates shared understanding and ownership among staff. Having everyone in the room discussing the organization's work, each department's contributions, and the outcomes you are all collectively working toward can be rejuvenating and inspiring. It allows everyone—even task-oriented staff or far-removed board members—to get a view of the big picture.

One of the most useful outcomes of a ToC process is how it forces you to examine your assumptions about how your organization is working to make impact. For example, you may be assuming that activity X leads to outcome Y, but do you really know? Have you proven that causal relationship? If you haven't proven it, that assumption is a risk. Once you have identified that risk, you can shore up that causal pathway.

A great example of this happened during the ToC process with another client—a local women's empowerment organization for underserved and underrepresented women, including those who have been incarcerated. As we were talking about how their food service certification (activity) leads to their program graduates getting jobs in the food industry (outcome), several staff raised the issue of employer hiring policies. Many local employers will not hire someone with a criminal record. This meant the organization's assumption that training and certifying women for the workforce was not sufficient to ensure they were employable; so they needed to revisit that assumption. They decided to add an activity to influence local employers to revisit their hiring policies to ensure the organization could meet the outcome of employment for their graduates.

Another useful outcome of building a ToC is that it illuminates what you need to be measuring. If you hypothesize that activity A leads to outcome B, and that outcome B contributes to your Bold Goal, what do you need to measure along the way to know whether that is happening? (Spoiler alert: If you haven't proven the causal relationships between activity A and outcome B, you need to measure that. If you have—and good for you—you now need to measure whether outcome B is indeed pushing toward your Bold Goal. Much more on measurement in the next chapter!)

For staff, building the ToC together also enhances transparency and accountability. They can clearly see how their day-to-day and month-to-month work contributes to the overall organizational hypothesis. They can also get a deeper understanding of why the organization is measuring certain things, like how many of their program graduates get jobs or how many employers change their hiring policies.

Lastly, the ToC allows you to consider issues outside your control. If your organizational outcomes are not sufficient, in the aggregate, to achieve your Bold Goal, you can consider what that means. Maybe you need to add more outcomes and activities to activate those outcomes, or maybe you need to partner with other entities that achieve outcomes that round out your Bold Goal. One common example of this is policy change. I have worked with several organizations that realized during their ToC building that their Bold Goal would not happen without policy changes. Generally speaking, their best options were either to partner with one or more advocacy organizations, hire a policy consultant, or begin planning to build a policy department.

In a perfect world, you would build an exciting ToC and then turn to strategic planning to lay out how you would make all that impact. We know the world is imperfect, though, so sometimes strategy comes before a ToC. No matter how you do it, what is most important is that you have both pieces, so let's discuss strategic planning.

BUILDING A GREAT STRATEGIC PLAN

Like *Alice in Wonderland* taught us, if you don't know where you're going, it doesn't really matter how you get there. Your theory of change shows you your destination, and your strategic plan is like a GPS system—you fix your destination and then explore various routes to get there. Without both, you can go really out of your way or even become totally lost.

Your strategic plan translates your ToC into how you will literally achieve your mission in the time period of the plan. (It used to be three- or five-year plans, but in this era of constant change those time horizons have been shrinking to one- or two-year plans.)

I have spent my career helping nonprofits be more effective through great strategic planning and implementation and execution. But don't just take my word for it. Several large studies have found a positive relationship between strategic planning and nonprofit performance. For example, the Association for Strategic Planning sponsored a large-scale survey of more than nine hundred American nonprofit organizations to explore the degree to which they apply strategic planning practices, as well as the relationship between these practices and nonprofit organizational success (Reid et al, 2014).

In a research report published about the survey in the journal *Strategy & Leadership*, the authors wrote, "If the goal is to raise the bar on nonprofit performance, we must equip all [nonprofit organizations] with the information and tools they need to meet higher standards of accountability and financial sustainability. To do this, they need a road map [ToC], a solid strategic plan, and a strategic management process that produces maximum benefits that can be implemented with limited resources" (Reid et al, 2014).

Two-thirds of highly successful organizations consider strategic planning to play a significant role in their success. Nonprofits that rate themselves as good at strategic planning delivered a more distinctive impact on their communities.

The research shows that well-formulated strategic plan development coupled with ongoing implementation oversight practices significantly influence overall organizational success (Reid et al, 2014).

The keys here are "well-formulated" and "ongoing implementation oversight." We are going to unpack "well-formulated" first (we'll get to implementation next).

Strategic plan development is both art and science. A good strategic plan includes priorities—aligned with your ToC—that indicate which activities and goals are most important, as well as metrics that indicate whether the organization is making progress toward its outcomes on the timeline of the plan. That is when it reaches what I like to call strategy nirvana, where literally everyone involved with the organization can make day-to-day and week-to-week decisions based on whatever their role is because they know exactly where the organization is going and how their work contributes to that bigger picture.

Unfortunately, strategic planning is not done well in many nonprofit organizations. In a recent study, while 90 percent of nonprofits surveyed engaged in strategic planning, the quality of the planning processes and the resulting plans were quite poor (Sargeant and Day, 2018). In my experience, poor strategic plans are generally vague and lack prioritization or good metrics.

Furthermore, staff are not routinely involved in the process or asked for their input. Many organizations do not use thorough environmental assessments or benchmarking data—two hallmarks of effective strategic planning. Less than half of nonprofit leaders surveyed were actually assessed against their plan during their annual performance reviews. Lastly, around 10 percent of boards of directors do not formally approve their organization's strategic plan (Sargeant and Day, 2018).

KEYS TO SUCCESSFUL STRATEGIC PLANNING
1) The Leader

In my experience, it is critical to have an internal person who is dedicated to thinking about strategy, herding the cats, and pushing the process along. I have seen failure occur when strategic planning and execution is yet another responsibility put on the plate of someone with too many other, competing responsibilities, like a COO or a VP of programs.

The dedicated strategy person is the lead shepherd of the process and the repository for all the research and stakeholder input coming in and being reflected in the draft plan documents.

To achieve this, hire or identify a big picture thinker. This person needs to value input, collaboration, and relationship building. He or she must be able to have relationships across the leadership team and the board of directors because this person needs to have access to information as well as the clout and gravitas to keep the process moving. This person also needs to have the patience, communications skills, and positive disposition to lead through times of volatility, uncertainty, complexity, and ambiguity.

Most importantly, this person needs to have the support of leadership and the board, because ultimately this person oversees the construction of the strategic plan that will be approved by both groups. If key members of the leadership team, including the CEO and the board chair, are not 100 percent supportive of the process, it will fail.

2) The Participants

One major mistake nonprofits make while strategic planning is limiting the participants involved in the process. Only 56 percent of nonprofits in one major survey indicated that "staff at all levels were involved in the planning process" (Sargeant and Day, 2018).

Robust strategies include input and feedback from a broad representation of stakeholders, including staff at all levels, board members, volunteers, program participants (those helped by the nonprofit), current and potential funders, current and potential partners, and other organizations in the ecosystem. The process is as important as the product, so the sooner the organization gets the people who are going to be contributing to the success of the plan involved with the plan, the more buy-in, enthusiasm, and collective goodwill there will be about the plan.

Many strategic planners—myself included—recommend setting up a steering committee to drive the planning process. Ideally, the committee will have representatives from your most important stakeholder groups (e.g. staff, board, sometimes funders or other external partners) and have a clear charter. Strategic planning steering committees often have the responsibility to consider data, draft strategies, and make recommendations, while final decisions are left to some combination of staff leadership and the board. The internal strategy person should manage the work of the steering committee, including setting up discussion topics and facilitating meetings.

Intentionally bringing in dissenters (i.e. problem children) is beneficial because when they are in the room, sharing and feeling heard, these naysayers often appreciate being included and also develop trust in the process. By including them, they can feel confident their colleagues are not only considering their viewpoints but also have a greater understanding of why those viewpoints may not be fully represented in the final product. One of my consulting clients has a vice president who had openly criticized the need for a strategy, so we invited him to be on the official Strategic Planning Steering Committee. At the end of the process, he was one of the biggest proponents of the final plan.

You also need input from external stakeholders, like current and potential partners, current and potential funders, or organizations that are good at the things that you need to do. For example, if you are a volunteer organization and there's another organization that really excels at utilizing volunteers, you might want to speak with them. Including subject matter experts is also useful. For example, at the National Alliance on Mental Illness (NAMI), we wanted to know how to be most effective in the advocacy arena, so we asked experts on Capitol Hill how our skills and influence were viewed, as well as what legislative opportunities would most benefit those living with mental illness. Speaking with academics, researchers, and scientists is an important way to collect information about levers that can be pulled to effect change.

Having a third-party consultant support you in your strategic planning process is often useful, particularly when you're collecting inputs where there may be issues of trust, skepticism, or negativity. When a third party is collecting data, the people who are providing the input feel safe to be truly honest and share their honest thoughts, ideas, concerns, and problems. Having that third party objectively analyze the data can also be beneficial.

3) The Timeline

Another mistake nonprofits make in strategic planning is not allowing enough time for the process. Nearly half of all organizations in the Association for Strategic Planning survey cited the lack of time to plan as a significant challenge (Reid et al, 2014).

Organizations commonly develop strategic plans during weekend retreats. As outlined above, having just one opportunity where stakeholders can contribute to strategy is problematic from a buy-in perspective. Additionally, it does not allow for different learning and participation styles. Not everyone is comfortable sharing and reacting to ideas in real time. Some people need more time to process, more time to think, and alternative ways of sharing their input and feedback. Also, developing a strategic plan in one shot can lead to "group think."

Afterward, as participants continue to think and reflect, they sometimes second guess those conclusions or have additional constructive ideas that are not reflected in the product. I have seen instances where staff return to the "real world" and realize some of those group think ideas are either not very strategic or impossible to execute. Hence, these weekend retreats tend to result in nothing other than a pretty chart to hang on the bulletin board.

Strategic planning is a fluid process, not a linear one; there are many "loops" when you draft, get feedback, iterate, get more feedback. You often take three steps forward and then one or two steps back. A thorough process includes time to listen, collect and synthesize insights, allow for a number of feedback loops, and bring everyone along in understanding the plan. It includes several rounds of synthesizing inputs, sharing that synthesis back with stakeholders and getting reactions, seeing what resonates, and seeing what feels feasible.

You also need time to socialize a lot of the pieces of strategic planning: making critical decisions about prioritizing what you do through a very intentional process about how we can have the greatest impact. Hard decisions take time!

Even a straightforward strategic planning process needs at least four to six months. This timeline will allow sufficient time for everything I described above. However, a massive undertaking like this needs to provide a solid timeline, clear expectations for those involved, and a time-bound "definition of done" in order to not lose momentum. You need to be intentional and transparent about who is advising the process, who is contributing to decisions, and with whom ultimate decision making ends. This is where a dedicated internal strategy leader could ensure everything stays on track and the organization does not lose focus.

Plenty of resources out there detail what a strategic plan should look like, so I will be really brief on this topic. Your final plan should be focused: three to five goals with three to five priorities under each goal (too many and you are not really focusing, are you?). Too many nonprofits have "everything but the kitchen sink" plans that try to be everything to everybody, but instead keep their resources spread thin and their impact solidly mediocre. Your plan should also include assignments for who is responsible for each piece, because accountability is key to success. Only 62 percent of nonprofits report clearly assigned staff responsibilities in their strategic plans (Sargeant and Day, 2018). Lastly, your plan should also include metrics that indicate whether you are making progress (we will discuss that more in the next chapter).

Once you have tackled "well-formulated," it is time to focus on "ongoing implementation oversight." Frankly, if you do not carefully execute and monitor your strategic plan, the time and energy you spent to create it was wasted.

How to Grow Your Impact

> ## How to Grow Your Impact:
>
> 1. Intentionally implement your strategic plan
> 2. Measure what matters

INTENTIONALLY IMPLEMENT YOUR STRATEGIC PLAN

A common yet harmful mistake nonprofits often make is to develop a strategic plan, hang it on the wall, put it on the website, and believe it will just magically happen. One study found that only 61 percent of nonprofits regularly consulted and amended their strategic plans (Sargeant and Day, 2018).

Another study by the Association for Strategic Planning found that 93 percent of the most successful organizations believed their ongoing implementation practices and evaluation have impact on their overall success. These practices include the leadership team monitoring and discussing progress at staff meetings, reviewing mission alignment at least annually, and reporting on progress regularly to both staff and the board. Moreover, the study showed that strategy implementation is an important differentiator between more and less successful organizations. Nonprofits assessed their own levels of success based on criteria like making distinctive impact in their communities, long-term sustainability, and steady funding (Reid et al, 2014).

Strategic plan implementation is its own beast and, in a lot of ways, much harder than developing the plan itself. It is not as easy as just flipping a switch and saying, "Okay, tomorrow is January first, the beginning of our new strategic plan, so we're going to start doing everything differently!" Does everybody know what they need to do differently? What new behaviors do we need to normalize? Does everybody know what new data needs to be collected? What processes need to be in place to collect those data? What are our talking points with partners, potential partners, clients, and constituents? How are we holding ourselves accountable?

Strategy implementation requires real focus on examining operations, processes, and behaviors in light of the new strategies and priorities. It requires patience and a genuine commitment to make changes if necessary—including tweaking, overhauling, or even eliminating certain activities or programs. It requires a backbone of steel to keep pushing forward instead of falling back on business as usual. It requires the time and sustained energy for true organizational learning and change. It requires hours and hours of meetings, conversations, communication, repetition, question-answering, strategy clarifying, pressure testing, frustrations, and epiphanies.

A shortage of financial and human resources is often a major obstacle to successful strategy implementation. In the Association for Strategic Planning survey, 54 percent of respondents said staff are spread too thin to pay explicit attention to plan implementation (Reid et al, 2014). In my experience, a lack of awareness about change management and organizational learning is also frequently a barrier. For example, after an arduous and expensive eighteen-month process to develop a new five-year strategic plan, senior leaders at one of my former employers believed the plan could be implemented by simply integrating it into the annual planning process without a focused implementation effort. Two years into the plan, the staff were still struggling to successfully execute it.

One way to help avoid failing on implementation is to recognize that it absolutely, on no uncertain terms, requires a dedicated staff person. This staff member shepherds the process along, leads strategy communications, drives learning and change, and keeps everyone in the organization accountable to the strategic plan. My recommendation is that this be the same person who led the building of the plan (see previous chapter).

For instance, my role at KABOOM! was to drive the implementation of the organization's brand-new strategy. My job was thinking about the strategy all the time and doing whatever it took for the organization to implement it. This included lots and lots and *lots* of communication: all staff meetings, board meetings, department meetings, office conversations, hallway conversations, ladies room conversations, memos, emails, etc. Experts call this "resolving the strategy," or achieving what I call "strategy nirvana" (see previous chapter).

Another must-do is to include milestones, timelines, and accountability in your implementation plan. You will need to "map and gap," which is to map your current activities to your new strategies to see what fits, what needs to be adjusted, what needs to be eliminated, and what new activities need to be added to mind the gaps. You will need to adjust operational processes, departmental plans, budgets, etc., in order to refocus your organization's operations on your new strategy. You will need to put measurement systems and practices in place to measure your progress. You will need staff tagged with specific responsibilities to ensure the work gets done.

Like I said, strategy implementation is a beast. There are a lot of moving pieces and truly tough decisions to be made. Losing momentum before you get to strategy nirvana is so easy.

Unfortunately, once you get there you can't really relax. A top-notch strategy is not a concrete thing, but a systemic and dynamic ideology that permeates all parts of the organization, from programs to hiring practices to culture. This ideology allows you to be both decisive and adaptable—both of which are critical to achieving impact. This means you can never take your eye off the strategy ball or get complacent about how your strategy is going. Measurement is essential to maintain your focus.

MEASURE WHAT MATTERS

The trickiest part of implementing your ToC and laser-focused strategic plan is measuring your progress. You need to assess whether what you are doing is having impact and measure how big that impact is.

Measurement is critical to our work in nonprofits for two other reasons as well. First, measurement data provide us with a feedback loop about how our work is going. Sadly, this doesn't happen as often as it should. A Stanford survey found that only 57 percent of nonprofits regularly use findings from their measurement and evaluation efforts to refine their ToC or strategic plan (Meehan and Jonker, 2019). Second, measurement data inform our decisions and helps us take calculated risks. Taking risks is one of the attributes of the more successful and resilient nonprofits (much more on this in Part 4). However, those risks must, ideally, be calculated ones. You cannot take a calculated risk without, well, the calculation you get from the data you collect.

There are actually a few different types of measurement you need to be doing. There are your big organization-level dashboard indicators, there are your more day-to-day program measures, and then there is periodic monitoring and evaluation. Let's talk about each of these.

ORGANIZATION-LEVEL DASHBOARD INDICATORS

Some people don't like the term "dashboard." I do. To me, it is a pretty good analogy for a summary of the most important pieces of information about how your organization is making impact, just like your car dashboard displays the most important pieces of information about your vehicle's performance and health.

As Share Our Strength cofounder Billy Shore told me, "Can you describe with real precision and clarity what success looks like for your organization? Once you do, almost everything else is derivative of it, everything else kind of falls into place, because it becomes obvious what you should be doing."

Your big organization-level dashboard indicators should begin with your ToC outcomes and strategic plan priorities. Your ToC outcomes and strategic plan priorities clearly define what success looks like. (If you don't have a ToC or a strategic plan, you should take a step back and clearly define what success looks like in some other format.)

Think about which pieces of information will tell you whether you are making progress on those outcomes and priorities. For example, at KABOOM! we arranged our dashboard by our five strategic pillars. One pillar was to increase play behavior in the communities in which we worked. Basically, we wanted kids to be playing more. Behavior is pretty difficult to measure, so we needed to carefully consider what we could actually measure, including what change could reasonably be attributed to our work.

With upstream efforts or more challenging impacts like behavior change, measuring success directly is often tough. In these cases, we need to rely on approximations, or "proxy" measures, that we believe correlate with more comprehensive success.

To develop KABOOM!'s play behavior dashboard measure, we needed to consider how we could collect data. Could we measure behavior directly in hundreds of communities through observing and measuring kids' play at school and at home? Probably not, since the staffing to do that would be prohibitively expensive. Could we survey all the kids in these communities about their play behavior? Unlikely, since we didn't really have a way of reaching them directly.

Or could we survey our community partners (schools, YMCAs, churches, etc.) with whom we were collaborating on building playgrounds and changing norms about the importance of play? Bingo. While the community partners' observations about play behavior was a step or two removed from observing it ourselves, it was a bit of a compromise. But it was the most realistic way for us to assess whether change was actually happening.

Big organizational-level measurements can evoke a lot of fear. Leaders may fear that measuring impact may show not enough impact for funders or general morale. Staff may fear that measuring outcomes may show they are doing something wrong or not working hard enough. When I was at the Corporation for National and Community Service (CNCS, the federal government agency that runs domestic service programs including AmeriCorps and Senior Corps), I led the development of the agency's very first set of performance measures. Some leaders and staff members were incredibly nervous about what the data would say and resisted the creation of the measures in both covert and overt ways.

However, you should not fear measurement. Measurement is your friend; it actually helps you do your job. It's like somebody whispering—or sometimes yelling—what's working, what's not working, what you need to keep doing, what you need to tweak. Shore put it very eloquently.

> *"Accountability is a really hard thing. I think there's a cultural discomfort in the nonprofit sector to being held accountable to specific goals. People are working hard, they're not paid as well as they should be, and they feel like 'why should I be judged when I'm doing my best and making sacrifices to do this work?' But from my point of view, the more you care about the work, the more reason you have to be held accountable. Accountability is not for donors or the board or anybody else, it's for the handful of people in the organization who are working their tails off and deserve to know whether they're allocating resources in the most effective way they can."*

A WORD ABOUT SHORT-TERM VERSUS LONG-TERM INDICATORS
Any problem worth solving is going to take a while. You may have the most amazing ToC with a snappy, ten-year Bold Goal and the programmatic chops to achieve it. However, maintaining enthusiasm and confidence when you are making progress for ten years is hard unless you have some reasonable shorter term measures in place. Short-term indicators are realistic, measurable, and tell you whether you are on track to meet your long-term indicators. Think of them as navigational aids.

Some nonprofits may never be able to truly measure their long-term impact. Some others may not know their impact until it is too late to course correct. For example, in *Upstream*, Dan Heath describes an initiative in the Chicago Public Schools (CPS). Its mission was to reduce the dropout rate, but the initiative couldn't wait four years (in which students would keep dropping out) to see whether its interventions were working. The initiative leaders needed shorter term indicators to guide their work. Academic research from the University of Chicago revealed that certain elements of high school freshman performance could predict which students were "on track" to graduate. However, even that was too long-term, because once a student is off track at the end of his or her freshman year, the damage has already been done (Heath, 2020).

CPS hypothesized that attendance and grades on a weekly basis were early indicators; that if it could boost attendance and grades, it could improve a student's freshmen "on track" standing, and that will boost chances of graduating. The leaders ended up proving their hypothesis and having tremendous success in reducing dropout rates (Heath, 2020).

As Heath said, "Getting short term measures right is frustratingly complex, and it's critical. In fact, the only thing worse than contending with short term measures is not having them at all."

A WORD ABOUT WHAT DATA LOOK LIKE

Not everything is a number. Sometimes what you need to measure is a process, an observation, or other pieces of qualitative information. My anthropology training taught me that observing data is extremely valuable, particularly when you are looking for changes in attitudes, norms, and patterns. For example, for my undergraduate thesis I interviewed about fifty Costa Ricans about non-Western medicine (e.g. medicinal plants, Santeria, witchcraft). I learned that the interviewees' expressions and body language as I asked certain questions helped me formulate a more robust characterization of their beliefs than I got from their words alone. I realized that questions about witchcraft made them really uncomfortable, which led me to do some additional research into cultural values that strengthened my project.

The flip side of collecting the data you need is *not* collecting the data you *don't* need. I spoke with one of my favorite measurement gurus, Saunji Fyffe, PhD, who has helped dozens of nonprofits evaluate their programs and measure their impact. Both of us have known many nonprofits that collect way more data than necessary. "When I see a list of one hundred key indicators, I have to believe they're not all exactly 'key,'" she said. Basically, do not waste time doing a whole bunch of data collection just for the sake of doing data collection. At CNCS, our first draft list contained about 230 performance measures; we eventually narrowed it down to seventeen measures.

The timing and frequency of when you measure your indicators is also very important. In the CPS example above, measuring graduation rate in September would not make much sense. You want to make sure that you have enough data to give you a good enough picture at the right point in time so that you can course correct if you are not on track. With that awareness, you can act more intentionally and effectively.

DAY-TO-DAY PROGRAM MANAGEMENT

You need to have a process for measuring how your programs are operating. This smaller-scale information acts as a navigational aid for your longer-term dashboard measures. You collect data that give you a clear picture of what is happening and look at the data periodically to give yourself enough time to really make changes.

Fyffe had the following pro tip regarding how to use your data: "Sometimes the data person puts the data out there but he or she doesn't know the meaning, and the people who would know what it means do not discuss it. Bring people to the table on a regular basis who can explain what's happening, have those discussions, and make any decisions you need to make about possible changes."

But who exactly should be at the table? "You want the key players, including leaders and anyone involved with implementation. Separately, leaders may not have the deep programmatic knowledge to interpret what the data mean, and staff on the ground may be too close to the work to see any trends that the data show," said Fyffe.

MONITORING AND EVALUATION

Monitoring and evaluation (M&E) is a somewhat different measurement can of worms. These are done periodically and usually by third party M&E folks who objectively look at your programs, systems, and data. Monitoring is used primarily to ensure compliance against a policy, grant, or contract to see whether or not an organization is doing what it said it was going to do. It is most common on really large-scale, government-funded programs, so I am going to stop there and talk about more common evaluations.

According to Fyffe, there are different levels of evaluation on a continuum. On one end there are very stringent evaluations of program impact, like randomized control trials, which evaluate progress against the ToC outcomes. On the other end of the continuum there are straightforward evaluations of program fidelity that evaluate how precisely and consistently your programs are being implemented. Evaluations generally occur every few years, or at various milestones in your strategic plan.

Any type of evaluation feeds into your dashboard and day-to-day indicators and vice versa. A program impact evaluation will give you information about how your ToC is working. A program fidelity evaluation will test the validity of your programmatic approaches and help you fine-tune your shorter-term indicators.

Some bizsplainers (those who believe nonprofits should behave like for-profits) are pushing evaluations on the stringent side of the continuum. Many believe that costly, lengthy impact evaluations and other similarly rigorous evaluations are the gold standard. Some large funders require and sometimes even fund lengthy evaluations. However, me, Fyffe, and many other experts in nonprofit performance measurement do not feel that expensive, elaborate measures and evaluations are necessary to know whether you are making impact. What matters is *what* you measure, not how much you spend or how fancy your collection methods are. We have all probably heard the term, "Garbage in, garbage out."

I don't care how much you paid for Salesforce. If you do not know what you need to be measuring and are not collecting the right information, all those bells and whistles are wasted. "Measurement doesn't need to be that complicated," said Fyffe. "It can be very simple. It doesn't have to be this complex, highly sophisticated system with the square root and all kinds of things." You can track your measures on the back of a napkin, just make sure that napkin has everything you need.

Once you are focused on making the biggest impact, you will need the right kind of leadership to make it happen.

PART 3

WE DON'T NEED ANOTHER HERO

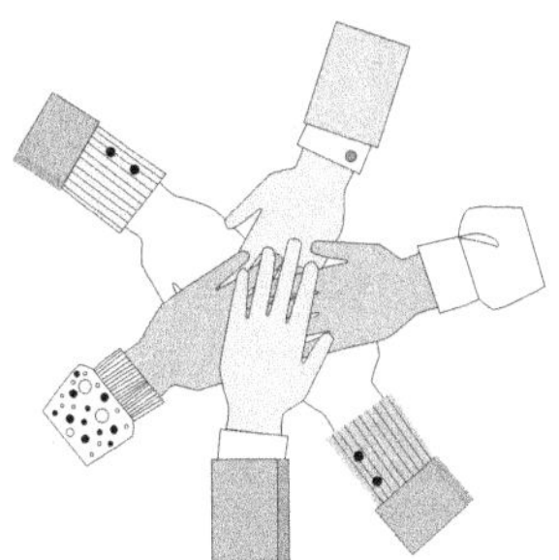

Other books say *visionary leader*; I say *sustainable leadership.*

We are obsessed with heroes. We love our superhero books and movies. We worship people who do big things, as well as superstar athletes, actors, musicians, and even those with the confounding title of "influencer." In fiction and in real life, we are always looking for someone to come save the day.

However, when it comes to what we are trying to accomplish as a nonprofit sector, all real societal changes have been achieved by groups of people and organizations. There are no singular heroes associated with these efforts, but instead teams of people collaborating toward a common mission.

I propose we shift our paradigm from leadership of a single flashy, charismatic "hero" (who is rewarded for ideas and charm with funding and celebrity) to one that values strong and sustainable leadership behind a focused plan (like those behind social impact successes like recycling programs or drunk driving laws).

In Part 3, we will investigate the fallacy of hero worship. We will consider what elements of nonprofit leadership are really needed and how staff throughout a nonprofit organization need to think and behave in new ways. We will learn about a more intentional approach to leadership development, as well as organizational structures that can support sustainable leadership.

Rethink Heroes

———

Heroes are often said to possess charisma, a word derived from the Greek phrase "divine gift of grace" (Riggio & Riggio, 2008), so perhaps it makes sense that humans see heroes as gods. The human tendency to assign god-like characteristics to heroic leaders can be traced all the way back to antiquity. The likes of Beowulf and Achilles were admired for their strength, courage, resourcefulness, and ability to slay enemies (Schein, 1984).

Every American knows the names and basic narratives of many heroes—both real and fictitious. "We're fascinated by people who do different things… strange things… [who] break the mold. We're fascinated by ordinary people dealing with extraordinary circumstances," says John Tomlin, executive producer of *Inside Edition* and *American Journal* (Shaw, 1994). The vast majority of our movie plotline tropes include a hero. We truly believe that one extraordinary human can lead followers to a new level of innovation, understanding, or peace.

Academically, the definition of hero has three parts. One, a hero takes action that is deemed to be morally good or that serves the greater good. Two, this good action is exceptional, not plain or ordinary. Three, a hero makes a significant sacrifice or takes a great risk in taking this good action.

Two leading hero researchers, Scott T. Allison and George R. Goethals of the University of Richmond, have written prolifically on why we're so enamored with heroes. To summarize their findings:

- Heroes energize us by promoting moral elevation, healing psychic wounds, inspiring psychological growth, and exuding charisma.
- Hero stories fulfill important cognitive and emotional needs, including the need for wisdom, meaning, hope, inspiration, and growth.
- Hero stories provide opportunities to learn by providing scripts for socially acceptable action, revealing fundamental truths about human existence, unpacking life's paradoxes, and cultivating emotional intelligence (Allison and Goethals, 2015).

Basically, heroes inspire us and motivate us toward our own personal growth and courage. We are drawn to heroes because of what they provide for us. We have all experienced the feeling of watching a movie and feeling inspired to do a good thing or motivated to take a risk. Personally, I remember practically sprinting out of the theater after seeing *Wonder Woman*, ready to fight to the death for honor and love.

THE MYTH AND FALLACY OF NONPROFIT HEROES

Currently, we have many nonprofits led by "hero" leaders conducting siloed efforts. A McKinsey survey asked about two hundred leaders of nonprofits, foundations, and social enterprises about their own skills and those of their peers. Sixty-one percent said too many leaders put the interests of their own organization ahead of collaborating with others. The same percentage said they see little cooperation occurring across the ecosystem. Only 11 percent said they or their peers are skilled in prioritizing problem solving ahead of organizational success; organizations would rather claim credit than contribute to a team effort that may solve a social problem (Callanan et al, 2015).

However, we have hard evidence that most major social changes have all been achieved by multiple, diverse groups of people and organizations. Real change is highly complex, contains many variables, and is driven by many forces; it requires our collective efforts. Therefore, could hero worship be a liability for nonprofits?

I spoke with Dan Cardinali, CEO of Independent Sector—an organization that guides and coordinates action across the nonprofit sector—who said, "Moving the needle is almost never one organization. It is always field building or eco-system ripening where a set of levers for social change can be pulled by multiple actors, sometimes the same lever and sometimes distinct levers."

He continued to talk about the challenges of a single hero leader. "I think we still innately default to the 'great person' leadership culture that holds out celebrities. However, problem solving necessarily requires a collegial or collective effort. So, we're looking for and rewarding the great leader and the great organization, and that's at odds with the actual collective action that is required," he said.

In her masterpiece book, *How Change Happens: Why Some Social Movements Succeed While Others Don't*, Leslie R. Crutchfield and her team at Georgetown University's McDonough School of Business Global Social Enterprise Initiative took a deep dive on fourteen US-based social change movements in the last forty or so years. The authors found that the most successful of these movements were not leaderless but "leaderfull," based on three principles of leaderfull social change movements:

- They empower local leaders to step forward, holding significant power in the grassroots.
- They feature broad coalitions instead of a single individual or organization making all the decisions and demanding credit. These coalitions often include both like-minded allies and "strange bedfellows." (We will talk a lot more about coalitions in Part 4.)
- They empower people with lived experience of the problem to speak and act on behalf of the cause (Crutchfield, 2018).

Another study of the fifteen greatest social impact stories around the world showed that nearly 75 percent of these impacts required coordination among key entities across multiple sectors (Bridgespan 2017). For example, the Tobacco Wars required scientific research and then collaboration among scientists, doctors, government leaders, and funders.

Bill Novelli, founder and former president of the Campaign for Tobacco-Free Kids and later CEO of AARP, was in the eye of that hurricane. He and his colleagues helped corral funders like the Robert Wood Johnson Foundation, coalition members like the American Cancer Society and the American Heart Association, and government leaders to fight the powerful tobacco industry and win (more on this in Part 4).

The same study identified three other patterns in massive social impact stories that indicate collaboration is advantageous:

- Social change usually takes a long time: nearly 90 percent of the efforts took more than twenty years.
- Social change frequently requires government cooperation: 80 percent required changes to government funding, policies, or actions.
- Social change often requires a major influx of capital: about 66 percent included one or more philanthropic "big bets" of $10 million or more (Bridgespan 2017).

What one name do you associate with fighting climate change or eradicating smallpox? The answer is there are no singular heroes associated with these efforts; they are leaderfull efforts of heroic people and teams working together toward a common cause.

Warren Bennis, a pioneer in the field of leadership studies who studied leadership for six decades, observed that you cannot lead if you do not motivate others and inspire trust. "Any person can aspire to lead," he says. "But leadership exists only with the consensus of followers."

Bennis's research found that all exemplary leaders have six competencies:

a. They create a sense of mission;
b. They motivate others to join them on that mission;
c. They create an adaptive social architecture for their followers;
d. They generate trust and optimism;
e. They develop other leaders; and
f. They get results (Bennis, 2007).

However, too many of the flashy, charismatic, solitary hero types I have known stop after (a). When they (b), it is usually just employees and funders, not necessarily other leaders or organizations. They usually dabble in (d), which really helps with the funding piece. However, they rarely (c), almost never (e)—which is tragic for our sector, and we'll talk about more in the next two chapters—and they (f) a lot less often than our hero myths would have you believe.

In my personal experience, a nonprofit founder I worked with was charming and charismatic with funders and partners but bullied his staff, which led to top talent departing and negative impact on partner relationships. Another CEO I worked with turned down an opportunity for a huge partnership with an organization she perceived as a competitor, instead of recognizing the potential to get a lot closer to going upstream and solving poverty in that community. Both leaders were ousted. Thanks to their flashy heroism, neither of them are currently supporting the missions they held so dear.

Crutchfield and her team also found that successful social change leaders realize that the true power is empowering other and that to succeed they need everyone around them to succeed. The founder of Ashoka, the international nonprofit dedicated to social entrepreneurship, Bill Drayton explained it this way: "We are living in a time of rapid change. We are moving from a world of silos and hierarchy to one of fluidity and many leaders."

This also means that vision and leadership cannot be the sole province of top executives. In this time of rapid change, vision and leadership need to be shared. One hero acting alone—making all the important decisions and expecting everyone to follow—is not the evidence-based way to achieve lasting social impact. The McKinsey study found that 53 percent of leaders said effective leaders must surround themselves with strong teams. Leaders with underdeveloped teams lack sounding boards for ideas and concerns (Callanan et al, 2014). Research shows that diverse groups that debate issues make better, more comprehensive decisions (more on that in the next chapter).

Effective nonprofit leadership is collective and collaborative and therefore strong and sustainable. Sustainability comes when information is held by a group of individuals and the culture supports ideas that come from anywhere in the organization. A nonprofit with strong, sustainable leadership has bench strength and is more than just a collection of assets. A nonprofit with that kind of leadership will be more effective in the fight to solve our biggest societal problems.

Since data show us that most successful social changes have been achieved by groups of people and organizations, we need leaders who can put ego aside and really focus on what works to solve these intractable societal problems. This means that tomorrow's nonprofit leaders need a whole host of qualities that are different from earlier eras.

Tomorrow's Leadership

Creating strong and sustainable leadership for radical nonprofit impact will require fresh approaches and new skills. Leadership is both the foundation and the roof of every great organization. But what does leadership even mean?

Simon Sinek refers to leadership as a social construct. He believes it is a choice, not a rank. "We follow those who lead, not because we have to, but because we want to," he said during his TED talk. Therefore, a nonprofit leader is anyone who has a role in decision making, whether that is from the board, C-suite, or at the department or team level. True leadership can come from anywhere. From here on, when I say "leader," I mean you.

Solving big social problems will require us to think and behave in new ways. Much like we are rethinking our definition of "leader," we also need to reexamine the qualities leaders need and the behaviors they must practice to be successful in today's nonprofit sector. As we discussed earlier, many of the old tropes about leaders no longer hold true.

Many books will tell you to emulate the for-profit sector, but I advise caution because some leadership attributes vary among the sectors. For example, competition is the norm in the for-profit sector, so skills related to successful competition are valued. As we now know, no nonprofit organization is able to achieve its mission alone, making collaboration and coalition-building more valued leadership skills in our sector.

Roselinde Torres, senior partner and managing director at the consulting firm BCG, surveyed hundreds of Fortune 500 companies. Torres identified three parameters on which we should be measuring our leaders in the twenty-first century:

1. Where are you looking to anticipate the next change?
2. What is the diversity measure of your network?
3. Are you courageous enough to abandon the past? (Or put more positively, are you courageous enough to adapt?) (Torres, 2013)

I realize that she surveyed leaders from the for-profit sector, but based on the nonprofit leaders I interviewed—as well as my own research and experience—I believe these parameters are also relevant to the nonprofit sector, with the addition of:

4. Do you intentionally create and model a culture of psychological safety in your organization?

Let's dig deeper on each of these four parameters of tomorrow's leadership.

ANTICIPATING CHANGE

Anticipating change is the active, intentional act of watching and listening for trends, patterns, and societal shifts that could impact your organization or communities. Your capacity to anticipate change is shaped by with whom you spend your time, what topics you follow in news and social media, and what books, periodicals, and podcasts you consume. Luckily, it is a skill you can develop and grow over time with practice.

James Siegal, former CEO of KABOOM! and also my former boss, said that one of the characteristics he has found in really successful, forward-thinking leaders is that they spend at least an hour a day just absorbing: reading something, listening to something, watching something. Often the expectation of senior leaders is to always be managing the organization, making decisions, building partnerships, getting funding, and building the brand. All of those are important, but the organization still needs that listening, trend watching, and anticipating function.

Without that ability to anticipate, organizations get stuck in operational mode. They hang out downstream, making small, reactive, incremental changes. They cannot see out of the tunnel to make proactive moves or educated bets on what will soon affect their organization or the people it is trying to help. They also remain beholden to old ways of doing things—and by extension the same old funding and funding cycles—because they are not thinking about how to get ahead of trends.

The interest in and capacity to anticipate change can come from any seat. If you see a pattern because you know people who work in XYZ and listen to a few podcasts on the topic, tell your boss, your boss's boss, the CEO, a board member, or anyone who will listen. For example, when a former colleague of mine saw the success a few other nonprofits were having with "birthday party" fundraisers in 2014, she suggested we design a simple template to encourage people to fundraise for us in that way. Now almost every nonprofit has a birthday fundraising program, but we were ahead of the curve.

CULTIVATING AND OPERATING WITHIN A DIVERSE NETWORK

Every human can benefit from surrounding themselves with people from diverse backgrounds with different perspectives, beliefs, and opinions. Most of us can also benefit from developing a capacity to form relationships with people who are very different from ourselves. As a nonprofit leader, cultivating a diverse network can benefit both you and your organization.

As we discussed in the last chapter, organizations benefit from diversity of thought. Many studies have shown that groups made up of people with different life experiences bring together many valuable perspectives, and diverse groups are better able to recognize problems and offer up creative and innovative solutions than groups of people with similar life experiences (Rock and Grant, 2016).

In *How Change Happens*, Crutchfield identifies "transcendent listening" as one of the most important qualities of a leaderfull leader. "Great movement leaders were able to not only hear, but deeply internalize and empathize with the others around them, both their closest allies as well as their adversaries and enemies," she wrote. An example she uses is Candy Lightner, the founder of Mothers Against Drunk Driving (MADD). Lightner intentionally made allies of those who were traditionally opposed to drunk driving laws, like law enforcement agencies and alcohol companies, because she was genuinely interested in hearing their perspectives (Crutchfield, 2018).

Beyond that, many other types of diversity should be considered: race, ethnicity, national origin, age, sexual orientation, gender identity, cultural/religious identity, physical and cognitive abilities/disabilities, and more. It's important for your staff to represent as many of those types as possible, especially those that are marginalized.

Nonprofits do not have a choice about "figuring out" diversity—we must. Solutions and programs need to be created *with* communities where we are trying to solve problems. Many organizations are struggling with what it looks like to have staff that represents those communities. There is also tension about how power is wielded and how decisions get made.

A recent study found that more than 80 percent of nonprofit staff recruit from their own networks. Unfortunately, these networks are not always diverse. For example, the study found that 75 percent of white Americans do not have any colleagues or friends of color in their networks (Fernandez and Brown, 2015).

A growing tension also exists between traditionally more conservative, older leaders and the typically more liberal, millennial and Gen Z leaders and staff—some of whom are both more attuned to the moral imperative around diversity and also more open to radical change. These younger professionals are speaking up and encouraging their underrepresented colleagues to do the same. Many millennial and Gen Z leaders are listening to these diverse voices, and it is changing the power dynamic for the better.

ABANDONING THE PAST AND ADAPTING TO MOVE FORWARD

"I believe adaptive capacity or resilience is the single most important quality in a leader," said Warren Bennis, pioneer of leadership studies. Adaptive capacity includes your comfort level with dreaming big, doing something different, and relinquishing total control.

DREAMING BIG

You may have heard of Dan Pallotta, founder of the Charity Defense Council and inventor of the multi-day charitable event industry, whose 2013 TED talk about nonprofit overhead went viral. He regularly pushes nonprofit leaders to be bolder, exemplified by his guest appearance on the nonprofit-focused podcast *We Are for Good.*

"I've been using the metaphor of prison: the nonprofit sector is in prison, and the for-profit sector roams free. Even when we [nonprofits] dream, we dream in miniature. We don't dream on the scale that Elon Musk is dreaming or Mark Zuckerberg is dreaming or Jeff Bezos is dreaming. These are people who lack any ounce of self-consciousness about the scale of their dreams, who come right out and say it, 'Colonize Mars, bring humanity to another planet.' But you try and get a person in a nonprofit to say it's their dream to end hunger in the city of Boston in the next ten years… They just can't bring themselves to think that big. It's 'hubris' to think that big. It's 'ego' to think that big."

Some nonprofit leaders do dream big. However, that level of unself-conscious bet-making is the exception, not the rule.

For example, George Vradenburg left a successful media career as a senior executive at AOL, CBS, and Fox to make a difference on an issue very personal to him and his wife Trish: Alzheimer's. The couple had been the cochairs of the National Alzheimer's Gala benefitting the Alzheimer's Association from 2003 to 2009 but were frustrated with the pace of the Association's pursuit of a cure. Trish's mother and grandmother had died of Alzheimer's, and the couple felt a real urgency to find a cure for the disease that could potentially affect her or their children (Weiner, 2021).

I spoke with Sally Sachar, the first COO of UsAgainstAlzheimer's, the organization started by George, Trish, and two other board members in 2010. She said, "They felt the space needed something disruptive and scrappy. They wanted to do advocacy, and they wanted to be much more aggressive in trying to get Alzheimer's funding increased."

The UsAgainstAlzheimer's team's lofty dream for disruption is paying off. It has increased the National Institutes of Health research funding for Alzheimer's from $440 million to more than $3.1 billion since 2010. This funding helped scientists discover that there are proactive, risk-reducing steps we can all take around diet, exercise, and social engagement to build resilience against cognitive decline.

Excitingly, in June 2021, the Food and Drug Administration approved the first ever disease-modifying therapy for early-stage Alzheimer's called aducanumab. "[This drug] is a dramatic turning point in the fight against Alzheimer's," said George Vradenburg in a press release. A few weeks later, two more drugs were submitted for FDA approval. "Just a few short weeks ago, Alzheimer's patients had no options at all for a treatment. Now patients have the approval of aducanumab as the first Alzheimer's therapy in nearly twenty years, with these new developments… offering new signs of hope on the horizon," said Vradenburg in a subsequent press release.

While these early-stage treatments are not cures, it certainly signals serious progress for this group of big dreamers.

DOING SOMETHING DIFFERENT

Kathy Bremer, managing director at BoardWalk Consulting, a national executive search firm that specializes in recruiting senior leaders for nonprofits and foundations, said that many nonprofits are looking for leaders who are risk takers. "An

organization that really needs big change will go for somebody that's quite different than an organization that needs
to build, maintain, or grow. The idea of a new leader who is
going to step out beyond the edge is big," she told me.

One leadership team that saw an opportunity to step out
beyond the edge to make bigger impact in the community
was the National Alliance on Mental Illness (NAMI) St.
Tammany of Mandeville, Louisiana. Since 1984, this nonprofit's mission has been to provide free education, advocacy,
support, and resources to anyone affected by mental health
needs. In 2013, Louisiana decided to close several state hospitals, including one in St. Tammany that housed people living
with serious mental illness. The state did not have a backup
plan for these individuals, so they would have become homeless. NAMI St. Tammany had not offered housing before but
was dismayed at the impact that the hospital closing would
have on the community.

The team centered on their mission. "We decided that if we're
truly here to help families and people living with mental
illness, how can we allow thirty people living with serious
mental illness just to be put on the street? So, we restructured
our organization for the well-being of those individuals and
the people in our community and took over from the state
housing program," said Nick Richard, NAMI St. Tammany's
executive director.

The organization immediately received backlash from both
the state, that did not want to continue funding the project, and the NAMI national office, that did not believe running a housing program was the right role for NAMI in the

community. However, almost ten years later, the NAMI St. Tammany Residential Community allows individuals who otherwise may be institutionalized or homeless to live in a less restrictive environment while preparing them to move in the direction of recovery and independence. NAMI St. Tammany provides qualified, trained staff including peer support specialists and caseworkers. To date, 140 individuals have been residents of the Residential Community, and many have been able to successfully return to stable housing outside of the program.

RELINQUISHING TOTAL CONTROL

For a traditional kind of leader, relinquishing control can be anywhere from mildly discomfiting to downright terrifying. I once reported to a CEO who would spend her valuable time copyediting our national organization's newsletters before they went out instead of trusting the communications staff. Unfortunately, top leaders not stepping back and having confidence that other staff will step forward is a major limiter on organizational impact.

Billy Shore and his sister Debbie founded Share Our Strength, the umbrella organization for the No Kid Hungry campaign, in 1984. This organization that began with a few hundred dollars and a desire to help victims of the famine in Ethiopia is now a powerhouse that raised over $160 million in 2020 to solve child hunger in the US. Shore's steady, understated leadership style is a big contributor to its success. US News & World Report named Shore as one of America's Best Leaders in 2005. He spoke to me about his leadership philosophy.

"One of the behaviors that I've always wanted to model is that at every inflection point in the organization, you need to slide down the bench a little bit and make room for other people. I think it comes fundamentally from the conviction that no one individual, no one organization, no one group of people is going to be able to end childhood hunger on their own; it's going to take hundreds if not thousands, or tens of thousands of us."

He clearly subscribes to the concept of leaderfull! I asked him how he had come to the idea of relinquishing control.

"One of the formative lessons for me was working for Gary Hart when he ran for president. For two years, I was sleeping on the floor of a friend's house and working on the New Hampshire presidential primary—which was the first primary and very important—and just giving up everything I had. The day he won the primary, the handful of us who had been responsible for helping him win that primary thought that we were it, that we had everything he needed. However, that was actually the day in which he needed more than we had to offer. We went from being a one-state campaign to a fifty-state campaign overnight, and none of us New Hampshire guys had experience in the other forty-nine states. This was a wake-up call that was really impressed on me. I've always thought about that at Share Our Strength as well."

In the last decade, Shore transitioned from CEO to chair of the board, as Share Our Strength hired a new CEO and other C-suite executives. His decision to share the power is one of the reasons the organization has continued to grow and thrive. For instance, Share Our Strength's No Kid Hungry campaign sent $100 million in grants to support local communities since the beginning of the pandemic. It also advocated to increase average SNAP (food stamps) benefits for families by more than 21 percent over pre-pandemic levels.

CREATING AND MODELING PSYCHOLOGICAL SAFETY

"I think psychological safety is one of the fundamental things that can help staff members understand their role in leading inside the organization, whether it's offering a suggestion, or challenging equity, or pushing back on an unreasonable expectation. Psychological safety is the fundamental thing to allow staff members more engagement in decision making, in equity, and in organizational change."

—ANNA PROW, FOUNDER OF TRELLIS PARTNERS

Psychological safety is the belief that you will not be punished or humiliated for speaking up with ideas, questions, concerns, or mistakes. Unfortunately, many people do not feel psychologically safe at work. According to analytics firm Gallup's survey data, three out of ten employees "strongly agreed" that their opinions don't count at work (Herway, 2017).

As leaders, it is absolutely, positively, unequivocally our responsibility to create and model psychological safety. This is strongly—but not exclusively—related to diversity.

A lack of psychological safety at a nonprofit has major repercussions for how effective the organization can be. For example, when people do not feel comfortable asking questions or expressing concerns about activities that are not working well, the organization is not equipped to be better. When the people who do not feel comfortable speaking up are the underrepresented voices, the organization misses the benefits of diversity of thought in problem solving and idea creation. A staff that disengages because their thoughts are not heard is not going to be the committed, creative staff you need to take the organization to the next level. (We will talk about taking risks and making brave decisions in Part 4.)

According to the Center for Creative Leadership, leaders can do the following to encourage psychological safety:

1. Make psychological safety an explicit priority.

Talk about the importance of psychological safety at work, connecting it to a higher purpose of promoting greater innovation, engagement, and a sense of inclusion.

2. Facilitate everyone speaking up.

Show genuine curiosity and honor candor and truth-telling. Model the behaviors you want to see by being open-minded, compassionate, and professional when someone is brave enough to say something that challenges the status quo or expresses ideas, questions, concerns, and mistakes.

3. Establish norms for how failure is handled.

Do not punish experimentation and risk taking. Encourage learning from failure and disappointment, and openly share what lessons you have learned from mistakes. (Much more on how to do this in Part 4.)

4. Create space for new ideas (even wild ones).

When challenging an idea, also express a larger context of support for having ideas. Consider whether you only want ideas that have been thoroughly tested, or whether you are willing to accept highly creative ideas that are not yet well-formulated, and express that expectation to your coworkers.

5. Embrace productive conflict.

Promote dialogue and healthy debate, and work to resolve conflicts productively. For example, you could discuss the following questions with your coworkers:

- How will people communicate their concerns about something that isn't working?
- How can questions or concerns about an idea or activity be shared with coworkers in a respectful manner?
- What are our norms for managing conflicting perspectives?

Tomorrow's leaders thinking and behaving in new ways can have tremendous positive consequences for our organizations. Fresh leadership skills can be the difference between mediocre impact and changing the world. But where do we find or how do we build these leaders? In the next chapter, we will explore the most important elements of leadership development.

How to Build Sustainable Leadership

> How to Build Sustainable Leadership:
>
> 1. Grow and support leaders
> 2. Structure for success

We have a retention problem.

Of more than 875 organizations in a nationwide survey of nonprofits, nearly all are experiencing staffing shortages (BKD 2021). High turnover has plagued organizations for decades. Turnover has increased since the beginning of the pandemic, and 42 percent of organizations expected the turnover rate to increase between 2020 and 2021 (Brew, 2021).

Baby boomers continue to age out of the workforce, but this is not the only reason talent is leaving our sector. Results from Nonprofit HR's 2021 Nonprofit Talent Retention Survey showed 46 percent of organizations reported the most challenge with retaining employees under thirty, 45 percent with retaining entry level staff, and 35 percent said mid-level staff—all groups of potential leaders (Brew, 2021).

Many people are seeking opportunities where they will not feel so overwhelmed, overworked, underappreciated, and underpaid. The primary reasons people leave nonprofit organizations are that a better opportunity presented itself (49 percent), lack of opportunity for upward mobility and career growth (44 percent), dissatisfaction or disengagement with current organization and culture (35 percent), and compensation and benefits (32 percent) (Brew, 2021).

Personally, I have known many nonprofit colleagues who left our ranks for jobs in foundations or the for-profit sector, where the hours are more regular, the stakes of the work are lower, the opportunities for advancement are clearer, and—let's be real—the salaries are higher.

When I say that the stakes elsewhere are lower, I am referring to how mentally grueling our nonprofit work can be. Day in and day out, we are facing difficult situations like abject poverty, crippling hunger, severely unfair oppression, extreme illness, and tragic loss. Solving really big social problems is exhausting and not always uplifting. We do these things because of the potential upside of making the world a better place, but the flip side can be a fair amount of anguish.

This exodus will only be exacerbated in the next several years, as nonprofits face increasing competition for leadership talent. The next generation of professionals are considering their career options right now. In today's information age, many of these young people are more savvy and worldly than those of us who came of age with word processors and dial-up modems. These future leaders expect real responsibility, mentoring, opportunities to advance, and meaning in their careers. We need to act now to attract and successfully retain our future leaders. The nonprofit sector may not have the same allure for mission-driven professionals as it once did, due to the increase in for-profit businesses with social agendas and new forms of do-gooding organizations (e.g., social enterprises, B corporations).

As mentioned in the last chapter, we also have a challenge with demographic diversity in our leadership pipeline. As Mistinguette Smith eloquently put it in a 2019 *Nonprofit Quarterly* article, "We are in a moment of seismic change. The fault lines are both generational and demographic. And nearly every organization has been hit by collapsing expectations and flying debris."

She went on to explain that many organizations pursued diversity without inclusion—hiring demographically diverse candidates but not assimilating or training them for leadership—leaving a void of BIPOC employees ready to lead. Worse, some of these would-be leaders are indeed ready, but the current leaders do not trust their skills. "Executives tend to mentor new leadership that looks and thinks just like them," she wrote. "These [current] executives are sometimes weary and ready to depart but unable to see the successors to whom they can responsibly pass the baton. Meanwhile, able candidates are weary of waiting for their turn to lead" (Smith, 2019).

As if this outlook wasn't bleak enough, the 2021 talent retention survey found that only 13 percent of nonprofits have a formal retention strategy.

All of this clearly adds up to problems for our nonprofit leadership pipeline. If baby boomers continue to retire and other leaders and would-be leaders leave for greener pastures but nobody behind them is prepared to lead, our ability to solve big social problems will be hamstrung.

But there are a few ways we can turn all this around. We need to invest more in the leadership development opportunities that yield the most impact for our emerging leaders. We also need to get creative about what leadership structures can push us further and faster.

GROW AND SUPPORT LEADERS

Part of our sector's leadership problem can be attributed to our miserable failure to develop our leaders. Several large, recent studies of nonprofit organizations found that most organizations are doing very little on leadership development. "Underinvestment in leadership also creates a cycle, a vicious one. Poor leadership development contributes to a range of mutually reinforcing problems: an inability to attract great employees, loss of employees, costly turnover, gaps in leadership... and burnout due to stress and the inability to do a job well. As a result, strong leaders are lost at a time when the sector needs them most" (Callanan et al, 2015).

A recent University of California, Berkeley study found that the social sector dramatically underinvests in leadership development compared with the for-profit sector. In 2011, the for-profit sector spent about $12 billion on skill development for its leaders, while nonprofits spent about $400 million in leadership development. The difference is stark: about $120 per employee annually in the for-profit sector versus $29 per employee in the social sector (Callanan et al, 2014).

The importance of our work to society and the emotional toll this work takes on us requires more development and support, not less. We need to be "leaderfull" to solve society's most intractable problems. With underinvestment in our leaders, it is no surprise we are struggling to meet society's needs.

Our leadership is also currently underperforming. The McKinsey leaders' survey found that across every category of leadership skill, leaders reported themselves and their peers to be deficient. The leadership skills they assessed included the ability to innovate, collaborate, and manage outcomes. Most leaders believe they lack the coaching, networks, and training they need to lead effectively (Callanan et al, 2014).

The leaders surveyed identified the top five attributes they believe leaders need. Dismayingly, leaders rank themselves and their peers extremely low on these five attributes. Across the five attributes, only 11 percent to 32 percent rated themselves as "strong" on each one. They rated their peers similarly, from 11 percent to 39 percent (Callanan et al, 2015).

(Which attribute was deemed as "strong" for only 11 percent of leaders, you wonder? "Places solving the problem ahead of individual/organizational success"—which underscores our flashy hero problem.)

Clearly, we need more leadership development, but what kind? The Center for Creative Leadership studied how executives learn for over thirty years and found that leadership is largely learned by doing. On-the-job learning has three times more impact on employee performance than formal training. Many organizations use what is called the 70–20–10 model as their blueprint for leadership training. As its name suggests, the model includes 70 percent on-the-job training, 20 percent coaching and mentoring, and 10 percent formal training (70–20–10 Rule 2020).

Humans retain information most effectively when we gain it in a practical context, and learning is even more powerful when we can have these practices reinforced in conversations with people who have done similar work. Likewise, formal training is most effective when it supplies technical skills, theories, and explanations that apply directly to our current experiences and are integrated quickly into our work (70-20-10 Rule 2020). Seventy percent of the leaders who responded to the McKinsey survey said they acquired their leadership skills on the job, and 67 percent said exposure to challenges and career transitions helped them grow (Callanan et al, 2014).

Unfortunately, in the nonprofit sector these development opportunities that can promote leadership skill enhancement are the most rarely available. Most reported leadership development opportunities were conferences, seminars, and subscriptions to professional publications—ones that don't correlate with performance improvements. To make matters worse, many leaders who *did* have access to rigorous leadership development like on-the-job training did not feel a genuine commitment from their organizations to make the most of the opportunities due to financial shortfalls and work pressures (Sargeant and Day, 2018).

This is likely because nonprofit organizations frequently have less support, structure, and supervision available for emerging leaders to take on a significant challenge. There are often fewer opportunities for mentorship due to the small size of many nonprofits and the burdens on top leaders. Nonprofits often have—or at least devote—fewer resources to formal training. Funders rarely prioritize leadership development in their contributions.

Sadly, sometimes nonprofit leaders are given "stretch goal" assignments without formal support or supplemental mentoring. These assignments then feel more like exploitation (more work with no pay increase) instead of development opportunities (Callanan et al, 2014). A former colleague of mine, who did not have people management experience, was thrown into a manager position when her boss got promoted. She was given no training or mentorship in management, which led to high stress levels for her and her team. She wound up leaving the organization after four miserable months.

This lack of opportunity to grow as a leader, along with the unavailability of mentoring and skills training, is a major cause of our leadership gap. We should also consider what nonprofit employees *want* in leadership development opportunities. The McKinsey leaders' survey shows these results:

- Forty-nine percent of respondents said they wanted time to experiment and innovate.
  - This sounds a lot like comfort with dreaming big and being willing to abandon the past—two new leadership skills we addressed in the last chapter. We will talk a lot more about risk in Part 4.
- Forty-nine percent of respondents said they wanted sabbatical time to rejuvenate themselves, gain exposure, and broaden their horizons.
  - I can personally attest to the value of a sabbatical, having taken a few in my career. Research backs me up: A 2009 study found that a sabbatical is not just a prime opportunity for the sabbatical taker to rejuvenate and grow, but it is also a valuable investment in organizational capacity because other staff can be given opportunities to stretch and grow in her absence (Linnell and Wolfred, 2010). On the other hand, it is also critical that employers value the past sabbaticals of potential new hires. Rejuvenating, getting exposure, and broadening one's horizons can all be beneficial when taking on a new position and should not be judged as a résumé "gap."
- Forty-two percent said they want opportunities for developing and accessing cross-sector networks.
  - This reflects understanding that nonprofit leaders must be skilled collaborators, work with multiple stakeholders who have diverse networks, and use sounding boards from other perspectives. We also talked about this in Chapter 3.2.

- Forty percent said they want opportunities for building communications skills, particularly media training and public speaking.
- Forty percent want coaching.
  - As an executive coach, I have had the privilege to help leaders develop various skills when they have the time and commitment to focus.

I would also be remiss if I did not mention compensation. In a 2008 Ready to Lead survey of nonprofit employees—including leaders and would-be leaders—69 percent of respondents said they were underpaid, and 64 percent said they had "financial concerns about committing to a career in the nonprofit sector." In a more recent study, 32 percent of employees leave their nonprofit organization because of compensation and benefits (Brew, 2021).

As leaders, we should be focused on leadership development to retain our best and ensure they are ready to lead.

STRUCTURE FOR SUCCESS

In today's era of rapid change, organizations in all sectors need to be more flexible and agile. Organizational structures may need to adjust so that leaders at all levels are enabled to be effective. Current structures are morphing, and new ones are being developed. To support strong and sustainable leadership, including leadership at all levels, a nonprofit organization needs to consider whether it has the right structure.

It's important to note that shifting organizational structure is a difficult thing to do. Our enduring constraints—money, staff, time, crushing community need—can keep us stuck in our ways. However, the potential payoffs are significant enough for us to carefully consider making a change. (More about how we can talk to our funders about supporting such changes in Part 6.)

TERM EXECUTIVE

The emerging term executive model provides change leadership for organizations to intentionally create the structures they need to carry on sustainable leadership and be effective at solving social problems.

A term executive is a time-bound nonprofit change leader who embeds with an organization during a period of transition and works with staff in every aspect of an organization's infrastructure to create conditions for increased impact. Term executives raise awareness of, and engagement in, a nonprofit's core functions, leadership, and culture. This engagement enables leadership and grows more leaders who can anticipate change, welcome diverse views, let go of unconstructive norms, and foster psychological safety while they tackle their missions.

This model was created by Anna Prow at Trellis Partners in Washington, DC. "It was important to design an approach that develops the wholesale readiness and resilience nonprofits need to make the bold moves essential for big gains," she told me. "A struggling nonprofit simply isn't equipped for the pace and intensity required to combat pervasive social inequity, and many nonprofit organizational challenges are a burden on the workforce."

Term executives appreciate that sometimes simple adjustments to nonprofit operations are not enough. They know that transformation takes time and investment, change efforts must be collaborative, trust is imperative, and team members must see their role in mission delivery. They use the opportunities that change can bring to strengthen what works and develop what's needed. A time-bound leader embedded on the inside can transform an organization's ability to set up the infrastructure, staffing, and culture needed to make real impact.

This model is a distinct contrast from the current common "fix" to support nonprofit change and growth: hire an external consultant. (Full disclosure, I have both hired external consultants and been one myself.) In my experience, the organizational needs that are best served by external consultants are those that are both concrete (e.g., a tangible deliverable like a report, new website, or social media marketing plan) and finite (e.g., technical writing for the report, coding expertise for the website, knowledge of social media best practices for the social media marketing plan).

However, short-term consultants are generally not hired to lead significant organizational change, nor are they usually in a position to institutionalize any of the work they do for the organization.

A term executive has many of the advantages of a full-time staff person—presence, trust, relationships, adaptability—at a lower cost and with no long-term commitment. He or she brings a unique insider-outsider perspective; the involvement is both deep and prolonged enough to be effective, without being so entrenched in the "we've always done it this way" attitude. The time-limited engagement is also short enough to create urgency and motivate action. Stakeholders can begin to see results in a short time. Unlike short-term consultants, a term executive is inside the organization to provide coaching and reinforcement of new behaviors and processes in an otherwise habituated culture.

To date, Trellis Partners term executives have helped more than a dozen visionary nonprofits scale and deepen their impact on a range of issues from expanding renewable energy, to achieving policing equity, to ending genocide.

TEAM-OF-TEAMS

Another emerging new structural model to ensure organizations are prepared for change is the team-of-teams model. Spearheaded by Ashoka, the international nonprofit dedicated to social entrepreneurship, team-of-teams is based on the principle that many important decisions require multiple inputs from different parts of an organization. No one function or department is likely to make unilateral decisions (Meehan and Jonker, 2019).

"The team-of-teams model emphasizes decentralized autonomy, meritocracy, and a sense of partnership. Teams come together around specific goals with a single coordinating executive team at the center, and the composition of each team shifts as needed over time. Teams and team members work together in constantly changing, fluid ways," write Meehan and Jonker in *Engine of Impact*.

Ashoka believes that all individuals can be agents of change, so the team-of-teams model allows for staff to lead in new and exciting ways. Staff also get the opportunity to use and showcase different skills on different projects. Hierarchies are broken down, and collaboration is easier as a result (Meehan and Jonker, 2019).

In an organization with a team-of-teams model, two-thirds of an employee's time might be on temporary teams created around a project, program, or outcome. This employee would have many on-the-job leadership development opportunities since her role would be different on each temporary team. She would be exposed to many more senior colleagues than she would in a traditional structure. Meritocracy is a critical element of this model, and this diversity of opportunities and exposure to senior staff would also give her more occasions to advance (Meehan and Jonker, 2019).

When Ashoka adopted this model internally, it had to radically shift its hiring practices. It now looks for characteristics (such as social and emotional intelligence) and impact on team culture (such as entrepreneurial spirit) instead of hiring for specific positions (Meehan and Jonker, 2019).

This paradigm shift is supported by the other current trends of technology and globalization. Some leaders believe that team-of-teams will grow in popularity in the nonprofit sector due to the nature of our work within a rapidly changing environment. On the for-profit side, many professional service firms, including management consulting firms, basically already use this kind of model (Meehan and Jonker, 2019).

THE STARFISH

An even more drastic example of an organizational shift is the starfish. Business leaders Ori Brafman and Rod A. Backstrom presented an interesting metaphor in their book, *The Starfish and the Spider: The Unstoppable Power of Leaderless Organizations*. To understand the metaphor, you have to grasp a little bit about how each creature works. A spider has a brain that functions as central command to control the movements of its eight legs, organs, and multitude of eyes. In contrast, a starfish has no brain and operates as a neural network of cells with no central command. When a starfish moves, scientists believe that one arm sends "signals" to the others to move the whole body. Each of its arms contains replicas of their major organs. If you cut off a starfish's arm, the original starfish just grows a new one (Brafman and Backstrom, 2008). (Fun fact: The severed arm could also grow into a brand-new starfish, since it has the organs and regenerative ability!)

To summarize, if you cut off a spider's head, it's a goner. A starfish doesn't have a head, but if you cut off any part of its structure, it will be fine.

Starfish-like organizations don't have a strong central command, but instead operate as decentralized networks where each area acts independently while coordinating with other areas as needed. These are known as relatively "leaderless" organizations (Brafman and Backstrom, 2008). Essentially, top leaders do not solve all the problems but instead create the conditions for staff to identify and solve problems themselves.

Proponents of this model believe a starfish organization is more resilient and adaptive. Intelligence is spread throughout the system, so it is able to respond more quickly because more people have access to knowledge and the ability to make decisions. It's able to mutate and innovate. It's also better for leadership development and employee engagement: when people are given trust and autonomy, they are motivated to contribute.

A nonprofit example of a starfish organization is Alcoholics Anonymous (AA). AA is not run by a leadership team. Instead, each chapter is run by members who are former alcoholics and relies on donations to cover its expenses. This decentralized structure seems to work very well: According to the AA website, AA currently has more than one hundred thousand groups, more than two million members, and continues to increase its number of chapters worldwide since its founding in the 1930s. Its structure allows AA to be flexible and constantly mutating.

In the next part, we will explore how this new kind of nonprofit leader can learn to confidently navigate risk to make brave decisions in the pursuit of solving our major societal problems.

PART 4

BRAVE NEW WORLD

Other books say *take risks*; I say *make brave decisions*.

There are thousands of books, articles, and podcasts about risk taking in business. There are slightly fewer on risk-taking in nonprofits. With risk comes the potential for failure—an f-word we often see as synonymous with "mistake" that can trigger emotions like hurt, anger, and shame.

According to Merriam-Webster, the definition of "bravery" is: "The quality or state of having or showing mental or moral strength to face danger, fear, or difficulty." Taking a risk in a nonprofit organization with limited staff and resources often means facing all three. It can cost us time, materials, money, credibility, social capital, and relationships with funders or partners.

In Part 4, we will study how some organizations confidently handle risk. We will explore what feels scary about collaboration for so many nonprofit leaders. We will learn how to strengthen our bravery muscles to make decisions that can lead to more effective approaches to solving our societal problems.

Learn from Science

———

I promised you I would not bizplain, but the for-profit sector knows that a business cannot grow or learn if it doesn't try new things and fail at some of them. Business people say, "Fail early, fail often," because they have realized that some of the most necessary lessons for businesses to succeed are nested in failure.

John Kern of Beta Strategy Group (and former principal at Community Wealth Partners) consults for both nonprofits and venture capital-funded, for-profit businesses. He explained to me how different the two groups' mindsets can be. "Even a well-resourced nonprofit will have a culture of scarcity and be really reluctant to spend money on anything, in part because it is focused on stewarding donor resources in the right way. My venture-funded clients have the same need to steward resources but there's a recognition that you spend the money to hire good people, and make ten bets and assume one is going to hit. It really allows people to do risky, innovative things," he said.

We have so many limitations on us in the nonprofit sector. We—rightfully—believe we need to be responsible stewards of our funders' and donors' money. Our resources are limited, and our funding seems precarious. We rarely have excess capacity, and the data we have to make decisions is often fuzzy or completely lacking. Unfortunately, this can lead to reticence or outright fear of trying new things and taking risks. We worry that failing will waste resources, hurt morale, or jeopardize our funding.

However, we nonprofits cannot afford not to take the risks. We absolutely need to learn the lessons that only risk and failure provide. If we can't try new things and grow, how can we possibly solve huge social problems? "If getting it tremendously right for the benefit of humanity means multiple times of getting it wrong first, it may be a risk worth taking," wrote social entrepreneur Tori Utley in an article for *Forbes Magazine.*

Risk is viewed differently in a science lab. There is an expected and acceptable risk involved with testing a hypothesis. In the lab, if your first hypothesis is wrong, the costs of testing that hypothesis might be time, materials, and money. You learn from it and move on to the next experiment.

I believe this inherent risk that is baked into the scientific method is worth exploring for building our nonprofit bravery muscles. Here is a story about how one nonprofit embraces the scientific method and has used it to make brave decisions to solve their chosen societal problem: cystic fibrosis. (Please note that the Cystic Fibrosis Foundation has been widely recognized for their extremely effective venture philanthropy model, but here I am focusing on how it has used scientific inquiry to make some key decisions over the last few decades.)

THE BEGINNING

According to the Cystic Fibrosis Foundation (CFF) website, CFF was founded in 1955 by parents who were watching their children die from a horrible disease. Doctors told them there was nothing anyone could do. At that time, the life expectancy for a child with cystic fibrosis (CF) was only about five years. This group of parents banded together and began raising money to change that reality.

In 1961, CFF established an accredited care center network and launched a patient data registry a few years later. By 1980, there were more than one hundred CFF-accredited care centers, and the median life expectancy for kids with CF had increased to eighteen years. CFF continued building a national network of care centers, supported a large number of researchers, and facilitated exchange of ideas and information among the researchers.

By 1989, the median life expectancy had increased to twenty-nine years. This increase was due to better treatments for symptoms and complications, like better lung clearance techniques, inflammation management, and antibiotic treatment. None of these therapies went upstream to the cause of the disease because it was not yet understood at its most basic level.

That same year, 1989, thanks to a big bet by CFF, a team of scientists discovered the defective CF gene and its protein product. This was a huge deal, considering it occurred years before the human genome was mapped. This discovery gave scientists much more information about the cause of the disease and lots of ideas of how they might address it.

Throughout the 1990s, CFF supported a great number of scientists working on the disease. CFF helped develop a new mucus-thinning treatment (Pulmozyme) to market in less than half of the industry average time. Researchers made progress understanding the gene mutation and the protein "folding" that cause CF but, unfortunately, found nothing close to a cure (Our History, 2021).

LEAP OF FAITH

After years of research, CF scientists now knew that a cure would require solving the protein folding issue that was defective with the mutated CF protein, but they had not figured out how to do that. I spoke with Bill Skach, MD, the chief scientific officer at CFF. He was a CF researcher in the nineties when scientists were just starting to observe that adding certain small molecules to cells might correct the folding problem. "The Foundation decided that if we just waited for the scientists to completely solve this problem, it was going to take too long. Let's take a leap of faith. CFF did something which was really quite controversial at the time; even many of the scientists disagreed with us," he said.

I asked him what CFF decided to do: "Based on laboratory data at the time, we thought there might possibly be a molecule somewhere out there that would fix the protein folding, and so the question became, 'How do we find that molecule?' CFF began funding molecular screening programs all around the country in which academic scientists and small companies would take millions of random small molecules and drop them onto cells. Nobody had any idea whether any molecule would work, but they just kept trying and seeing if one would make the protein function better. It was this huge leap of faith."

I wondered why this experimentation was controversial. Skach answered, "Because there was a general belief you needed to understand the problem in order to solve it. If you didn't understand the problem, you might just be wandering in the darkness. The molecular screening programs were trying to solve a problem that we didn't really understand; it was really just a hope that there might be a small molecule out there that could be turned into an effective drug. At the same time scientists were working on understanding the basic folding problem, we added on this new molecule discovery component which was trying to leapfrog over what we didn't know yet. Both groups began working together to find a solution."

While the screening programs and scientists continued to find and better understand new types of molecules, CFF also began setting up a network of academic research centers that would be ready to conduct the clinical drug trials which would be needed if the right molecules were ever found. They also raised money to support all of this and supported development and approval of several other treatments that eventually became available to people with CF (Our History, 2021).

A true breakthrough occurred in 2006 when one of those random molecules was successfully identified and eventually led to development of one of the first oral drugs that worked at the cellular level and attacked the root cause of CF, and that drug entered clinical trials.

Over the next fifteen years, multiple drugs that treat the underlying cause of CF were approved by the FDA and today provide tremendous therapeutic benefit for more than 90 percent of people living with CF. In addition, virtually every approved drug available today for treatment of CF was made possible in some manner by support from CFF. According to Dr. Skach, "Each new breakthrough brings us closer to our vision of a cure for all people with CF." Since CFF began in 1955, the median life expectancy for people living with CF has risen from five to fifty years (Our History, 2021).

CFF has a strong foundation in science, in part because it has kept scientists on its staff and board for decades. I asked Dr. Skach how CFF views taking risks: "When you're trying to go into an unknown area, you never know what is going to be successful; that's the nature of the unknown. I think we funded about twelve molecular screening programs, and only one has successfully brought drugs to patients to date. The failures were just part of the course. We took a chance, it didn't work, so we needed to take another chance."

This nonprofit almost out-scienced the scientists when it jumped over fully understanding the protein problem to experimenting with small molecules. Not every scientist agreed with this approach; however, the organization's staff was willing to take that leap of faith and see how it went.

"If the molecule screening hadn't worked, we would have stopped that and gone on to something else. But when you see progress being made, then you continue down that path and continue to exploit all the tools available," said Skach.

"The nature of science is that there's this discourse for disagreement, and there is also a way to resolve those disagreements. That is the scientific method. It's perfectly okay to have scientists disagree, but the scientific method will ultimately lead you to the right answer if you continually apply it in a careful, meticulous manner," said Skach. "Scientists who are unable to change their mind are generally very poor scientists. We will always need strong opinions and strong scientists, but if you're really smart, you can admit you're wrong when the data prove you're wrong," he concluded.

This is a nonprofit organization that took a risk, expected some of its efforts would fail, and made a brave decision to continue down that path. We can all learn from the Cystic Fibrosis Foundation's bravery to go further and faster toward a cure. More of us need to push ourselves and our organizations toward risks, bold decision making, and potential internal disagreement—even if it's scary—if we want to find the "cure" for our own missions.

Collaborate Creatively

"To collaborate with another person is to admit weakness. There's no way of getting around it. If you weren't in a position of weakness, you wouldn't need anyone else's help. When engaging in a collaboration, you're saying, 'I don't know how to do this on my own.'"

—ROSS MCCAMMON, BUSINESS ETIQUETTE
COLUMNIST AT *ENTREPRENEUR MAGAZINE*

Seeing collaboration as admitting weakness is likely hardwired for some of us. Collaboration brings up all kinds of anxieties, like "Why can't I accomplish this alone?" or "What will happen if we can't get along or are not successful?" or "Will we get blamed if our efforts or ideas don't work?"

However, history has shown that no one hero or heroic organization can solve our huge societal problems alone. The reasons for us to partner with other people and organizations significantly outweigh the drawbacks, so we need to get past this already.

There are a few basic forms of collaboration among nonprofits and other entities, like for-profit companies and government agencies:

- There are partnerships, where two or more entities agree to cooperate to advance their mutual interests, such as amplifying reach or solving a problem from multiple angles. For example, a social services nonprofit might partner with a food bank to sign people up for SNAP (food stamp) benefits when they come pick up donated food.
- There are coalitions, where two or (usually) more entities agree to work together to achieve a common goal, such as passing a bill or eliminating a disease. For example, according to their 2021 report, the coalition partners of the GradNation campaign have increased the US high school graduation rate from 71 percent in 2001 to 85.8 percent in 2019.
- The most dramatic form of collaboration is a merger, where two entities are legally consolidated into one. Keep reading for an example of a successful merger.

Specifically due to the COVID-19 pandemic, uncertainty of funding and skyrocketing demand for their services drove organizations to seek new ways to continue operating. The BKD "State of the Nonprofit Sector" Annual Report revealed that in 2021, 16 percent were seriously considering some type of partnership, 13 percent a strategic alliance, and only 9 percent a merger.

Nonprofits are reluctant to collaborate with other nonprofits for many reasons. Nonprofits balk at collaborating with for-profits and government entities for many more reasons.

WHY NONPROFITS ARE RELUCTANT TO COLLABORATE

IDENTITY

Every nonprofit I have ever worked with believes it is unique. "No other organization does what we do, how we do it, has the relationships we have, or helps people the way we do," we think. Similarly, "Someone outside our organization cannot ever fully understand us and certainly cannot tell us what to do. Therefore, if we were to collaborate with others, we would be 'giving something away' or 'losing ourselves' in the process." There is a reflex to protect the brand and a sense of responsibility or obligation to hold what we do as sacrosanct. When it comes to collaborating with for-profit businesses, the feeling of compromising our identity or reputation as mission-driven as opposed to money making is even more worrisome.

EGO

With (thankfully) few exceptions, every nonprofit leader wants to make a positive impact. Boards and senior leadership feel like they know what they're doing. They believe they know how to build something meaningful and change people's lives. It is human nature to want credit for doing something good. Not everyone wants to share the spotlight. This goes quadruple for nonprofit founders, who often feel they deserve the credit because of the blood, sweat, and tears they put in to start the organization.

COMPETITION

The competition for support and attention is getting more heated. The abundance of nonprofits means that many are chasing the same funding. Nonprofits are also competing for brand awareness, and they are not just competing with each other for that; they are competing with for-profit businesses as well (more on this in Part 5). Competition can sometimes push nonprofits to differentiate themselves instead of collaborating.

TRUST

Related to competition, but also separate. Some leaders are not comfortable sharing proprietary brand information, data, or even internal "dirty laundry" with other organizations because they do not trust it will not be used against them in some way. For example, a nonprofit might be reluctant to collaborate with another organization if it means that the partner would see how scant its data is or how its board is under engaged.

FEAR OF CHANGE

Humans typically fear change. We fear the uncertainty it brings. "Human beings like the world to be just, orderly, and predictable so we know how to behave," said Gail Sahar, professor of psychology at Wheaton College. "It is quite anxiety provoking to be uncertain because the right course of action is unclear. It makes us feel insecure and unsafe." Sahar believes that the search for certainty is probably rooted in a basic biological survival instinct (McKeon, 2021).

Uncertainty also feels scary because it includes the potential for loss—in this case, loss of power, territory, status, credibility, even the loss of your job. Having managed many change processes in various organizations, I can tell you that a person's fear responses can kick in especially powerfully when they fear their job description, title, or status might change. I've been yelled at more than once, falsely accused of all kinds of things, and had people beg me not to include a certain strategy or performance measure in a strategic plan.

One of my favorite instances was when I was told I was the "[Expletive] high priestess of the [expletive] strategic plan who can just shove it up your ass," by an irate coworker as he stormed out of the meeting room and slammed the door. Approximately ten other colleagues in the room and I all just blinked a few times and then carried on with the meeting. Later, one of them commended me for not bursting into tears. I think the key is to remember that it's not personal, that people can be fearful in the face of uncertainty; though, I must admit it's tough to handle sometimes.

WHY NONPROFITS ABSOLUTELY NEED TO COLLABORATE

In *How Change Happens: Why Some Social Movements Succeed While Others Don't*, Leslie Crutchfield and her team identified the common characteristics of successful social movements such as preventing drunk driving, preserving gun rights, and achieving marriage equality. These successful movements invariably required going upstream (which we talked about in Part 2), having inclusive and ego-free leadership (which we talked about in Part 3), and for reckoning with adversarial allies. Success happened when leaders forsook organizational identity and the need to get credit, and instead worked together toward a common goal.

MAXIMUM MISSION IMPACT

Organizations that find ways to collaborate in truly strategic ways can have more impact together than they would have as separate entities.

For more than a century, cigarettes and other tobacco products were virtually unregulated. Because tobacco was identified as neither food nor drug, it was not subject to the Food, Drug, and Cosmetic Act of the Food and Drug Administration (FDA). This status was largely due to the money and power of the tobacco industry, which continued to be exempted even as the dangers of tobacco products were scientifically documented and the industry's deliberate techniques to assure the addictive properties of its products were exposed (Chambers, 2017).

In 1995, the rate of adult smoking had fallen from 43 percent in 1964 (when the first Surgeon General's report on the dangers of smoking came out) to about 25 percent. However, the rate of high school kids smoking was rising. As Bill Novelli wrote in his book *Good Business: The Talk, Fight, Win Way to Change the World*, "It was a national crisis; and a whole generation of kids was at risk."

A large-scale effort was needed to take on the powerful tobacco lobby. One important lever was FDA Commissioner David Kessler's claim that regulatory oversight over the tobacco industry should be under the purview of the FDA. President Bill Clinton was very supportive, as were other government leaders, including Donna Shalala, C. Everett Koop, and key members of Congress. Several state attorneys general had begun to file lawsuits against the tobacco industry as well (Novelli, 2021).

Novelli and his team played a huge role in assembling a broad coalition of organizations, influential individuals, and funders for the Campaign for Tobacco-Free Kids, initially supported by the Robert Wood Johnson Foundation. Novelli, founder and president, assembled a team of experienced people and brought together major anti-tobacco players like the American Medical Association, the American Cancer Society, the American Heart Association, the American Association of Family Physicians, and the American Academy of Pediatrics. The coalition also pulled in powerful individuals, trial lawyers, philanthropists, and big funders like the Annie E. Casey Foundation and the Conrad N. Hilton Foundation (Novelli, 2021).

Within the next fifteen years as the lawsuits worked their way through the courts, tobacco companies agreed to pay about $206 billion over twenty-five years to compensate for smoking-related medical expenses, as well as fund programs to reduce smoking among kids. The FDA was given oversight over tobacco. There are now bans on smoking in enclosed spaces in many cities, and rising tobacco taxes are increasingly used to discourage smoking (Chambers, 2017).

Youth smoking rates fell from 25 percent of high school students in 2000 to 6 percent in 2019. "Millions of kids will not become addicted smokers, and many millions of adults will not die prematurely of tobacco-caused disease," wrote Novelli (Novelli, 2021).

I asked Novelli about his collaboration strategy. He told me, "The trick is not to ask, 'Who can I partner with today?' The trick is to ask, 'What do I want to accomplish?' and then, 'Who does that lead me to partner with?' Maybe it's a strange bedfellow or somebody I don't like."

MOVING UPSTREAM

Like we talked about in Part 2 on Focus, we nonprofits should be going upstream toward root causes and solutions whenever we can. Collaboration with other entities with complementary missions or capacities can be an excellent way to address those root causes.

One example comes from KABOOM!, the national nonprofit dedicated to play. The "influence strategy" we developed to create better play infrastructure and impact the lives of more kids required the organization to take a major partnership risk. Municipal (city and town) governments are where infrastructure decisions get made, so going upstream meant influencing them. We had historically avoided partnering with municipalities because of both bureaucratic red tape and the potential political implications for us and our funders. In comparison, the contractual requirements and timelines of entities like schools, churches, and other community groups were simpler, so we mostly partnered with them to build our playgrounds.

Deciding to start partnering with municipalities was also risky because we had been avoiding them for fifteen years. Some of them may have a problem based on KABOOM! previously just coming to town with a single playground project and then leaving. We were not sure what they thought of us, nor how they would react when we suddenly said we wanted to work together. Building the first partnerships with New York City and Baltimore was certainly challenging. We needed to hire new people who had experience working with cities. We had to forge relationships with the right staff in those city government structures. We had to adjust our operations and budgeting for longer and more complicated contract negotiations.

James Siegal, KABOOM!'s former CEO and current senior advisor, spoke to me about how the process is going.

"We did not overestimate the challenges of partnering with municipal partners. It can be more challenging to work with them, but the upside is so much greater in terms of scaled solutions and potential impact. So far, we've made some significant changes to demonstrate that we can partner effectively with municipalities and that bigger change is possible. We haven't gotten there yet, but the potential transformative change is right ahead of us now. Under CEO Lysa Ratliff's leadership, we've just launched an ambitious new initiative to eliminate playspace inequity in twenty-five places in five years. This is a solvable problem at scale, and the new kinds of partnerships we are forging

*with municipal agencies, communities, and funders are
essential to get there."*

ACHIEVE GREATER EFFICIENCY

With something like 1.5 million nonprofits in the United
States today—and more forming every day—it stands to
reason that there is a considerable amount of overlap in
missions and communities we are helping. Each nonprofit
has a unique blend of skills, capacities, relationships, and
funding. Getting closer to solving a problem may mean that
two or more nonprofits should merge, demonstrated in the
following example.

Founded in 1988, Metro TeenAIDS (MTA) addressed the
severe HIV/AIDS epidemic in the National Capital region
by focusing on the needs of children and youth, providing
services for HIV prevention and HIV/AIDS treatment in the
Washington, DC, area. It was, at one time, the largest HIV/
AIDS youth organization in the world.

I spoke with Adam Tenner, former executive director. Under
his leadership, MTA experienced tremendous growth in both
programs and revenue between 2003 and 2013. However,
beginning with the stock market drop in 2009, the organization was facing major changes to its funding landscape.
There were projected changes in the national HIV and public
health funding landscape and health care delivery due to the
Patient Protection and Affordable Care Act (also known as
Obamacare), as well as change brewing in local fundraising circumstances.

Tenner and his team became very uncertain about the organization's sustainability. "As an executive director, you think your role is to untie all the knots. I got to a place where I couldn't untie the knots," said Tenner.

Anticipating those changes, Tenner worked with the MTA board and staff leadership to identify options, ultimately deciding that the best way to continue serving DC area youth was to join forces with a Federally Qualified Health Center that could bill Medicaid and insurance for services and provide seamless integration of HIV/AIDS prevention and treatment.

Among the leading candidates for a merger was Whitman-Walker Health (WWH), a Washington, DC, nonprofit community health center and a national leader in HIV/AIDS services. Tenner noted there was good strategic alignment because WWH had hoped to expand its services to youth. MTA's programs became part of WWH in February 2015. Tenner's proactive approach helped ensure that all of MTA's programs could continue while extending WWH's reach to young people.

This merger was so successful in preserving the value to the community that the national nonprofit AIDS United commissioned a report on the process entitled "Is It Time to Close?" This report was designed to help other organizations—specifically those engaged in HIV/AIDS—make decisions about their own sustainability.

"If you care about the mission, purpose, and people you help, I think it's unethical not to consider the options to partner or merge. If you believe in what your organization is trying to accomplish, you have to consider how collaboration could lead to delivering more impact," Tenner concluded.

These success stories are hopeful, and every single one took courage. You may be wondering if you or your organization is brave enough to collaborate in big, meaningful ways. Can just anyone learn to make brave decisions?

How to Make Brave Decisions

How to Make Brave Decisions:

1. Create a supportive environment for trying new things
2. Explore new ways to collaborate

"Let urgency conquer fear. The time to take action is now. Not tomorrow. Today. Develop a sense of urgency about the issue, because a sense of urgency is often the only thing that drives us to find time to make change."
—JEAN CASE, BUSINESSWOMAN AND PHILANTHROPIST

We know that getting closer to solving big societal problems will require us to do different things, and some of these things may be risky. However, as Case said, the stakes are too high for us to sit back and continue making incremental progress. Humans are adaptable, and we can all learn to be bolder and braver.

CREATE A SUPPORTIVE ENVIRONMENT FOR TRYING NEW THINGS

"When you create a learning environment where smart people can take smart risks, you open your nonprofit up to finding the next win."

—PAMELA BARDEN, NONPROFIT FUNDRAISER

For your organization to improve at making brave decisions, two things need to happen. First, you need to ensure that your people are in—or can spend some time in—the right mindset. Second, you need to have an organizational structure or process through which to experiment, fail, learn, and move on.

One rubric for thinking about comfort with risk and failure is "fixed" versus "growth" mindsets. A person with a fixed mindset has rigid beliefs about intelligence and skills: either you have them, or you don't. As you can imagine, a fixed mindset limits a person's ability to learn and grow because she essentially does not believe anyone *can* do that. She focuses on performance instead, and her evaluation of others is limited to first impressions and performance (Gino and Staats, 2015).

On the other hand, a person with a growth mindset believes that she can improve and learn with effort and practice. She seeks challenges and learning opportunities. She is able to persist past obstacles because she does not see failure as a sign of inadequacy. Obviously, she is also much more comfortable taking risks (Gino and Staats, 2015).

I discovered another way of thinking about how people view failure that expands the fixed versus growth rubric. Author, professor, and neuroeconomics expert Baba Shiv has his own description:

- The Type 1 mindset is fearful of making mistakes. In this mindset, failing is shameful.
- The Type 2 mindset is fearful of losing out on opportunities. In this mindset, sitting on the sidelines while someone else runs away with a great idea is shameful.

We usually have adventurous Type 2 mindsets as children. But as we grow older and more self-conscious, and if life tells us repeatedly that failure is shameful or not allowed, we convert to Type 1 (Shiv, 2011).

Start-up companies in places like Silicon Valley are full of Type 2s. In Type 2 cultures, failure is not bad. On the contrary, failure can be super exciting; it could lead to an "aha!" moment of insight that could be your next great idea (Shiv, 2011). These companies expect failure and even prepare for it with the help of internal "fail fests" and public conferences like FailCon.

But most nonprofits have very different cultures than Silicon Valley. We have cultures where taking risks and failing is unacceptable, and we often don't have the structures to evaluate lessons learned from things we have tried.

Would you believe me if I told you there is an organization that helps you fail? Fail Forward is the world's first failure consultancy that supports people and organizations to fail intelligently. The people at Fail Forward believe that "intelligent failure is a learned skill that everyone can practice and strengthen." Growth mindset, exhibit A! They say that building the skill of intelligent failure takes practice, and they're here to help ("About Us" 2022).

Fail Forward's founder and CEO, Ashley Good, used to be a development worker with Engineers Without Borders Canada (EWB). EWB pioneered the concept of a "failure report," a glossy document published every year containing real stories that offer insight into individual and systemic failures and lessons learned from each one. EWB was trying to break down the stigma that surrounds failure in the nonprofit sector because it was frustrated by the learning opportunities that were missed as a result (Brown, 2017).

These failure reports hit a nerve. In a sector where looking good means getting funded and looking bad may mean closing your doors, we are not used to talking about failure. We are beginning to try it; nonprofits have begun embracing internal "fail fests" and even the occasional external conversation about what didn't work.

Fail Forward's website says that to get better at intelligent failure, you must:

1. Detect and accept failures quickly. Ideally this is a collaborative process where you engage your staff to collect all the hypotheses you hope to test. Clearly define every

new idea to be tested with a short, written summary of the concept, budget, timeline to implement, expected outcomes, and potential risks (Case, 2019). Clarifying what lessons you are hoping to learn is also helpful. Having good data, like we talked about in Part 2, is really helpful when deciding what to test. Your data can tell you if a new idea has a decent chance of succeeding based on what you know now and what you can predict down the road (Barden, 2010). Baba Shiv and others recommend something called "rapid prototyping," where you brainstorm new ideas and then quickly move from the abstract to the concrete in mocking up the new activity or program. Some experts recommend creating a specific process—and even a related funding pool—for taking risks that is separate from other departments and budgets. We did this at KABOOM! and called it our experimentation fund.

2. Analyze what happened and how it happened to maximize learning. Track and document what you learn from each new idea with a formal final evaluation, including thoughts about how to tweak it (what not to do) next time (Barden, 2010). Each failure rules out something that doesn't work and brings you a step closer to the next big idea.

3. Apply learning to change mindsets, behaviors, and the way we work. Take what worked well and integrate it into your current programs, design the next experiment, rinse, and repeat. It's important to note that experts warn us not to try too many experiments at once, because having too many new things happening at the same time makes it difficult to discern what results came from which experiment.

4. Continue taking smart risks and innovating, ensuring we make better mistakes on our next attempt. Taking risks and learning from failure can cultivate courage and bravery. With teamwork and a well-structured process, your collective mindset can shift from associating failure with shame to associating it with excitement and progress.

People can change their mindsets! They sometimes just need a little help.

Ideally, all your activities should reinforce learning and growth. Leaders can set the example with how we talk about learning new skills—both as individuals and as an organization. Employee performance reviews can evaluate efforts to learn in addition to the usual performance metrics. It's worth mentioning that you can make organizational risk taking go a little more smoothly if you evaluate candidates for hire or promotion on their growth mindsets.

EXPLORE NEW WAYS TO COLLABORATE

Genuine, productive collaboration takes courage and time. In our fast-changing world where we want to make big impacts, it often also takes creativity.

KNOW YOURSELF

Collaboration must enhance your ability to deliver on your mission. In Anna Prow's experience as an executive and term executive at many nonprofits, an organization must know itself first in order to know how it can be a part of a partnership or coalition. She says, "It's got to know what its strengths

are. It's got to know what its weaknesses are. It's got to have
a clear strategy. It's got to have effective leadership. It's got
to have all that stuff underneath it so that it can go fully to
another group and say, 'Okay, here's what we do well. Here's
what you do well. Let's join up together and do this other
thing.' And then the organization has to have the resilience
to hold firm and be a good partner."

One way to do this is to conduct a self-assessment. In this
process, you assess your key organizational challenges and
critical issues, identify potential gaps or needs you will need
to address to succeed, and consider how a potential partnership might enhance or weaken any competitive advantages
(Brenner and Heyman, 2019). If any of these areas prove to
be problematic, you'll want to correct them and create the
right conditions for partnership first before approaching
another organization.

You also need to formally assess potential partners. Are the
partner's mission, vision, and programs compatible or complementary with yours? What are the partner's strengths and
weaknesses? What is the partner's financial situation, and
how does it relate to yours? Is there trust? Are the cultures
compatible? Together, you and your partner(s) will need to
resolve how decisions will get made, as well as who will ultimately lead (Brenner and Heyman, 2019).

An example of when an organization truly "knew itself"
while assessing a potential partnership was one opportunity
presented to the Spitfire Club, a local nonprofit of which I
am currently the board chair. The Spitfire Club is an extra-
curricular book and girls' empowerment club built around

children's books featuring strong, diverse, female protagonists. When a recent partnership opportunity came along, the timing was perfect: We had just completed a strategy refresh where we had specifically considered which girls we wanted to be reaching and had renewed our focus on girls who face structural and systemic barriers to literacy, visibility, and opportunity.

We were approached by a charter school that wanted to offer Spitfire book clubs as part of its afterschool program. This bilingual school had a mission that seemed well aligned with ours. Parents paid for the afterschool programming, which meant that the school could pay us a fee for our service. However, when we dug a little deeper into the logistics, it seemed that our clubs would only be populated with girls whose parents could pay, which meant that the girls we were truly trying to reach—the ones with the structural barrier of having parents who could not afford the program—would once again miss out on an opportunity.

Walking away from good money was tough, but we decided that our missions were not truly complementary, and this collaboration would have compromised our values.

TAKE ADVANTAGE OF TIMING

Collaboration also requires a sense of timing. Dan Cardinali, of Independent Sector, tracks movements and collaboration within the sector. "There are disproportionately important moments when an organization can leverage its voice, competency, thought leadership, and practice that can be market

making or field building. You can feel that something is ripening," he told me.

During the consumer movement of the 1960s and 1970s,
safety standards was a major theme. For example, Ralph
Nader's 1965 book, *Unsafe at Any Speed*, about the unsafe
vehicles produced by the American automotive industry, was
a significant force behind the passage of the 1966 National
Traffic and Motor Vehicle Safety Act. The act set mandatory
federal vehicle safety standards and established a federal
agency to enforce them (Jensen, 2015).

However, if you purchased a car that had a manufacturing
defect, the manufacturers almost always failed to honor
their warranties and fix the problem. Aggravated car buy-
ers usually either gave up and sold their "lemons" at a loss
or covered the repairs out of pocket. Millions of consumers were plagued by unrepairable cars and unresponsive
automakers. In 1979, California resident Rosemary Shahan
had had enough. Her car dealer had had her car for three
months without repairing it. Frustrated, she began picketing
outside the dealership. The dealership threatened to have
her arrested, but other consumers were taking notice and
joining the cause. She continued protesting and picketing
for five months.

I spoke with Shahan about her timing. "The car manufacturers and dealers were really ruining people's lives. These
were honest, hard-working people who hadn't done anything
wrong. All they did was buy a car, and they relied on this car
to get to work, to get their kids to school, to get groceries. I
was hearing from consumers. They had cars where the brakes

didn't work, or the steering would go out. Just terrifying. They were afraid to drive them. People were going back and back and back to the dealers, and the cars were in the shop all the time."

I asked her what the automakers' response had been. "California's warranty law at that time gave auto manufacturers a 'reasonable number' of repair attempts before they were required to give lemon owners a refund or replacement vehicle," she said. But what was "reasonable"? At a legislative hearing, a representative from Ford Motor Company testified: "There are times when thirty visits might be required to fix the problem." No wonder consumers were demanding change.

In response, Shahan founded a nonprofit organization, Motor Voters—later renamed the Consumers for Auto Reliability and Safety (CARS) Foundation—and enlisted fellow consumer advocates in San Diego as board members. They raised small donations from irate lemon owners and mobilized with media, letter writing campaigns, coalition building, and testifying at hearings in Sacramento.

"To get to lawmakers, you need to activate their constituents," said Shahan. However, collaborating with the media proved extremely difficult, because automakers and dealers were some of the media outlets' biggest advertisers, and they withdrew advertising in order to pressure news organizations not to cover consumer news like this.

"People were losing their jobs. I talked with reporters who were in tears, who said, 'I can't do the story.'" However, one by one media outlets began to stand with the CARS Foundation against the unrepentant automakers. "I give the media a lot of credit for covering the issue and making people aware, to the point where politicians felt some pressure," said Shahan.

The CARS Foundation worked with California lawmakers, including Bill Lockyer and Sally Tanner, for several years to get a "lemon law" passed, despite vehement opposition from auto manufacturers. Finally, it passed overwhelmingly in the state legislature and was signed into law in 1982. The landmark consumer protection law created a legal presumption that four tries to fix a major problem—or thirty days out of service during the first twelve months or twelve thousand miles—was enough to trigger the auto manufacturer's obligation to provide a refund or replacement vehicle. "When it passed, it was wildly popular. Our bill became the model for laws in all fifty states. Connecticut actually beat us to the punch; they read about the bill and passed one before California did," Shahan recalled. "Legislators were falling over themselves to introduce bills because consumers everywhere were angry."

Lemon laws give consumers legal remedies for defects covered by an auto manufacturer's warranty. Thanks to Shahan and her coalition of consumer advocates leveraging the automobile safety consumer trend, today lemon owners have lemon laws on their side.

TAKE ANOTHER LOOK AT YOUR ISSUE

Especially when we think in upstream ways, we'll find that our work often intersects with organizations that work on different, but related, issues. It requires courage to consider something bigger.

One example is Share Our Strength, which doubled down on childhood hunger twelve years ago when it developed its No Kid Hungry campaign and has been laser-focused on ending childhood hunger in America ever since.

"I think the biggest challenge we have right now as an organization is acknowledging and acting on the learning that even if we're 100 percent successful on everything we're doing—school lunch, school breakfast, and summer meals—it won't be enough because you can't end childhood hunger in a sustainable way without addressing poverty. That's a big change for us—this notion of getting to some of the root causes of why people are hungry in the first place," Billy Shore told me.

I asked him what exactly his organization was doing differently: "It requires us to think a lot more expansively. For example, some of my colleagues are strongly urging that we get involved in affordable housing issues, because affordable housing has so much to do with the disposable income of low-income families."

The National Alliance on Mental Illness (NAMI) contends with similar challenges in getting involved with the different yet related issue of law enforcement. NAMI envisions a world where all people affected by mental illness live healthy, fulfilling lives supported by a community that cares. Unfortunately, our current justice system too often wrongfully punishes and incarcerates people who are living with mental illness. While the organization's main focus is on education about and care for mental illness, from its inception in 1979 NAMI has also had to advocate for appropriate and just policies in the justice system.

CONSIDER STRUCTURE

Successful collaboration may require new ways of thinking about structure that are less siloed. Some new organizations are embedding collaboration into their organizational design. One example is the Peacock Rebellion in Oakland, California. On its website, this collective calls itself "a SF Bay Area-based, queer and trans Black, Indigenous, and people of color (QTB-IPOC) crew of artist-activist-healers."

Adam Fong of the Hewlett Foundation told me more about the collective. "It was started by queer and transgender BIPOC artists. In response to some transphobic things that occurred in their comedy training program, it shifted the next iteration of the program to be exclusively by and for transgender BIPOC artists—with a production crew that was majority transgender BIPOC—and began shifting the organization to be majority trans BIPOC led. As it evolved, particularly in response to the Trump administration, it started to serve as a rapid-response network for trans people in its community. It built out partners in health. It built out partners in transportation. It partnered with a bike shop and other tenants and residents to launch the first queer and trans BIPOC-centered land trust with permanently afford-able housing—all these really unexpected things that are very customized to the people it is trying to support," he said.

There are also new types of collaborative structure being utilized by entities focused on community wealth building that do not look like traditional nonprofit organizations, built with governance that has local control. These are cropping up everywhere, and the fertile Bay Area is no exception. "We're seeing lots of interesting stuff around land trusts, community ownership, and linking 501(c)(3)s with other forms, whether it's local community developers or (c)(4)s [a kind of nonprofit organization that can engage in political campaigns] to push for legislation that improves the functioning of the government," said Fong.

CROSS BRIDGES INTO THE FOR-PROFIT SECTOR

We know that identity and trust can be challenges in considering collaborations with the for-profit sector, and it takes bravery to overcome our reservations. However, there are huge opportunities for true collaboration and innovation, and for using their financial and human resources to advance our missions. Recently, market forces, including the pandemic and ongoing racial justice movement, have pushed for-profit companies to rethink their role in creating positive social good.

For example, like we covered in Part 1, social service nonprofits have been advocating for a living wage for decades, but only recently are more retail workers being paid fifteen dollars an hour. The change occurred because the for-profit companies that hire these workers finally responded to economic conditions or social pressure. This act of social good is a victory for retail workers, and its impact is a good example of why nonprofits may want to reconsider collaborating with for-profit entities.

Our long-held beliefs about the division between for-profits and nonprofits are crumbling. Much has been written about nonprofits seeking opportunities for earned revenue, like selling products at local retailers. For example, one of my clients trains women in food service and baking, and then sells the cookies and granola the women make through their training programs in local stores. This is an excellent way to get unrestricted funding. Unfortunately, not all nonprofits produce sellable goods.

Luckily, such goods are not the only avenue to partner with our friends in the money-making sector. A lesser-known method is when a nonprofit organization sells products or services to *for-profit companies* instead of consumers. This model offers win-win-win scenarios: the company wins, the nonprofit wins, and society wins. It's not exactly B2B (business-to-business) as they say in the for-profit world… instead it's N2B (nonprofit-to-business).

For example, Rare is an international nonprofit organization that drives social and behavioral change for people and nature in sixty countries. According to its website, Rare looked at publicly available data and saw that many Americans want to do more to fight climate change but don't know where to start. It also found employee engagement data showing that nearly 60 percent of job seekers and more than 75 percent of millennials care about a company's social and environmental commitments. Many job seekers and employees would like their employers to offer sustainability programs.

Rare recognized a gap between what employees want and what's available to them, as well as an opportunity to help employers attract and retain top talent. The organization created an environmental employee engagement service called Green Benefits to sell to employers. Green Benefits incentivizes employees to take climate and sustainability actions, like reducing food waste, adopting renewable green energy sources, or purchasing an electric vehicle. In this model, an employer wins (engaged employees who feel good about their company), Rare wins (behavioral change on environmental issues plus unrestricted revenue for its mission), and society wins (more people being intentional about their impact on the environment) (Make it Personal 2021).

A more localized example is the Literacy Council of Northern Virginia (LCNV), which recently began offering local employers onsite English as a Second Language (ESL) classes for their employees. I spoke with Roopal Saran, LCNV's executive director. "There are a lot of employers in this area that hire recent immigrants. We have gone directly to these employers and said, 'You run a hotel. You need your employees—bellboys, housekeeping staff, kitchen workers—to be able to have certain interactions with your guests. I remember hearing an example where a guest asked the housekeeping staff person for another towel, and the housekeeper turned around and left to go get it, without saying, 'I'll be right back,'" she said.

I asked her how exactly the revenue model works. "We have the employer pay us to offer a customized ESL class for its employees, onsite, however many classes it wants. The employer can make it a perk, make it an employee benefit, whatever. We will bring our teachers and work with their supervisors to understand the specific conversations they want their employees to be able to comfortably have," she explained.

Again, an employer wins (employees are better able to communicate with customers and are potentially more loyal to the company), LCNV wins (community members' lives are improved, plus unrestricted revenue for its mission), and the employees win (increased opportunities from better mastery of the English language).

Our nonprofit sector's mission is too important to let fear hold us back. As Siegal told me, "You have two things existing at the same time. You've got the fear of change because it could get worse. And then you've got the fear that if you don't change, it will get worse. Those are both constants." Don't wait for fear to subside, but bravely make decisions today that could lead you to have more impact tomorrow.

PART 5

TAKIN' CARE OF BUSINESS

Other books say *act like* a for-profit business; I say *borrow what's relevant* from for-profit business.

If I had a nickel for every time I've heard or read, "Nonprofits should be run like for-profit businesses," my nonprofit salary would have been supplemented quite nicely over the last twenty years. Most nonprofit management books are filled with for-profit business management principles slightly revised for nonprofits. However, the purpose, funding, and impacts of nonprofits are all fundamentally different from for-profit businesses, so why do we believe they should operate the same way?

Investors of for-profit businesses expect financial returns on their investments, while funders of nonprofit organizations expect "social return." While businesses measure things like sales and market share, measuring nonprofit missions and impacts is usually not as quantifiable or easy. Furthermore, what motivates people in the nonprofit sector is not fame and fortune (or at least it shouldn't be; see Part 3), so our incentive structure is also very distinct from the for-profit sector.

Given these vast differences, I propose that we only borrow what we really need from the for-profit sector and not the whole enchilada.

In Part 5, we will take stock of which for-profit practices are most current and relevant to our sector. We will consider the unintended effects of our more relaxed nonprofit workplace cultures. We will discuss our current approach to branding and marketing. We will learn how we might emulate for-profit best practices in accountability and branding to advance our missions.

Professionalism

"Culture eats strategy for breakfast."
—PETER DRUCKER, LEGENDARY MANAGEMENT GURU

What exactly is culture? This anthropologist is glad you asked! Culture is really about people. The anthropological definition of culture is shared history, values, and practices. In a workplace, culture refers to the beliefs and behaviors that determine how the people there interact with one another and outside stakeholders (like partners, volunteers, and program participants). It's also what the organization does for its employees and what the employees do for their organization.

Workplace culture is generally a combination of aspects that are shaped intentionally and those that arise organically, and it affects every aspect of an organization's operations, from hiring decisions to dress code to office design to employee benefits. Culture is the glue that either holds everything together or keeps the organization stuck in unproductive or even toxic patterns. Workplaces that understand the power of culture are intentional about designing theirs.

First and foremost, a workplace culture should focus on how to interact professionally and collegially. This allows us to get our work done while ensuring our coworkers and other people we interact with feel respected and continue to work with us. In the for-profit world, the saying is "time is money." However, there are a lot of other professional behaviors that translate to making money. Building good relationships is money; think about sales, promotions, partnerships. Clear communication is money. Hiring the right people with the right skills and mindset for the job is money.

Bill Novelli was a bona fide corporate, Madison Avenue "ad man" before he turned his talents to social marketing in the nonprofit sector. He had run a huge portion of CARE and led the Campaign for Tobacco-Free Kids before coming to AARP as an SVP and then CEO. At that point he had decades of nonprofit experience, but sometimes his for-profit reputation still preceded him.

"Cultures are so different," he told me. "At AARP, I used to do 'Breakfasts with Bill' with staff from all over the organization. I remember this one young woman saying to me, 'I think you're making us too corporate.' I said, 'What do you mean?' She said, 'I'm afraid we're going to lose our sense of mission.' Mission is so critical to nonprofits; that's why the people get up and go to work, and that's what they care about."

What that young woman was alluding to in her conversation with Novelli is that nonprofit workplace cultures often look very different from for-profit corporate cultures. Nonprofits tend to be less rigid, less formal, and more "family-like." We also—as we talked about in Part 2—often have less-defined business goals and measures of success. While for-profits measure things like sales targets, market share, products produced, customers retained, and money made, our day-to-day raison d'etre can be much fuzzier. This can make accountability a challenge for nonprofit workplace cultures.

Let me insert a caveat here: I have spent more than twenty years working in and around dozens of nonprofit cultures. I have not spent much time working in for-profit cultures. I cannot honestly say that every single nonprofit has problems with professionalism. I also cannot say that every for-profit corporate culture nails it. However, I can authoritatively say that many nonprofits suffer from letting casualness, the emotion of the work, and—let's be really honest—the feeling that we don't get paid enough to follow rigid rules and protocols get in the way of truly professional and accountable culture.

WE'RE NOT FAMILY

What we do in the nonprofit sector—working on gut-wrenchingly sad, hair-pullingly frustrating, and primal-screamingly unfair social problems—is demanding and takes an emotional toll. Our more casual nonprofit workplace cultures can reflect the nature and difficulty of our work and are intended to be comforting, but a corresponding lack of professionalism could be holding us back as a sector.

In your time in and around nonprofits, you have likely heard some version of "We're not just coworkers; we're family!" For-profit companies place less value on a family vibe and more on their business goals. Sure, the workplace is more pleasant if you enjoy your colleagues, but clear for-profit business goals take precedence. While your nonprofit workplace can be a safe space where you have warm, supportive relationships with your colleagues, it does you a disservice to think of them as family.

Alison Green, author of the popular *Ask a Manager* blog and book of the same title, is concerned that "family" is being used to pressure and exploit nonprofit staff. "'We're like a family here' tends to be used in ways that really disadvantage workers," she wrote. "It often means that boundaries get violated and people are expected to show inappropriate amounts of commitment and loyalty, even when it's not in their self-interest. In practice, the companies and managers that say this are usually dysfunctional. Work works best when each side has healthy boundaries in place" (Herrera, 2018).

Denise Lee Yohn, brand leadership expert and author, laid out several reasons why your workplace is not like family:

- Unlike in a family, the people in your workplace are working together to accomplish a goal.
- Unlike among family members, power dynamics, expectations, responsibilities, and accountability are well-defined among people in your workplace.
- Unlike a family, a workplace has performance standards.
- Unlike in a family, people decide (or are told) to leave a workplace.

An important part of a healthy workplace culture is psychological safety. We talked about this in Part 3, but briefly it's the belief that you won't be punished or humiliated for speaking up with ideas, questions, concerns, or mistakes.

Unfortunately, some families are not psychologically safe environments, so we do not want to emulate that in the workplace.

WE'RE NOT HERE TO PLAY GAMES

Many nonprofit organizations have culture leaders or "captains" who try to make the experience a little more fun. These well-intentioned individuals understand that morale is important and that we need some levity in our workplaces to offset the seriousness of the work we do. However, when the culture-building is limited to fluffy team-building exercises, happy hours, potluck holiday lunches, and bowling outings, it actually may undermine our effectiveness.

Liz Ryan, a former SVP of human resources at Fortune 500 companies, puts a fine point on it in an article she wrote for *Forbes Magazine*, "Team-building exercises are pointless and even insulting to your team members, because they suggest that if only your team members spent more time doing silly things and solving group problems together, climbing trees and rolling around on the floor, they would work more effectively together the rest of the time. When a team hasn't gelled and isn't communicating, it's not because they need team-building training. It's because there is a problem, and no one is talking about it."

Ryan puts the blame on leaders for not recognizing or not being willing to address the problem head on. "There are real business issues getting in the way of your team's performance, as well as your own, and dragging everybody to the high school rock climbing wall will not address those problems," she wrote. "No one ever hired a consultant to put on a team-building workshop when there were no problems! We only think about team-building when the team isn't working together well. That's a leadership problem."

Team bonding has benefits, but not if it is only masking real issues. I completely agree with her aversion to "forcible team building" because I have never seen it fix any workplace problems. Do we bond with our coworkers and get to know them as actual people? Sure, it's definitely nice to connect with other humans and learn about their fear of heights or love of German shepherds. But does that translate to them being less aggressive or territorial or obstructionary in our next meeting? Not in my experience.

GENERAL NASTINESS

"Toxic" workplace culture generates a lot of buzz, and I posit that the toxicity arrives and thrives because we are too light on professionalism and accountability. I have seen or heard about a number of other unprofessional behaviors in many nonprofit workplaces that are caused by an inattention to accountability.

In a for-profit business, accountability is more clearly tied to tangibles like sales and revenue. For example, you may have to make five hundred widgets this quarter, and your team has a collective target of ten thousand widgets. Your numbers are tracked and publicly acknowledged, and you know that your compensation—and maybe even your ability to keep your job—is tied to those numbers. In a nonprofit, our goals are more intangible like creating a program or establishing a partnership. You can measure whether you have created a program, but how can you tell if it was done in the most efficient, effective way that has the biggest impact in the community? Accountability here is murkier.

Nothing breeds discontent like lack of accountability. Without accountability, nobody can count on anyone else or trust them to do their part. Nobody is engaged, and therefore nobody is invested in the outcome. Nobody can expect to be recognized or rewarded for hard work. It is doubly damaging when leaders are not held accountable for leadership responsibilities—not just performance goals—like clear communication, delineation of roles, and team building (6 Pitfalls 2021).

Tolerating poor performance is an issue across all sectors, but our fuzzy notions of accountability can mean we do it more than most. Ignore low performance issues at your peril. In a survey of more than 1,700 professionals from all sectors, 68 percent of respondents reported that low performers hurt morale in the workplace and increase the workload for others. Fifty-four percent of respondents said that low performers stifle innovation. Their lack of initiative and motivation contributes to a workplace culture where mediocrity is accepted (Eagle Hill 2015).

To make matters worse, the tolerance of poor performance can also drive your top performers away.

Other problems due to an inattention to accountability:

- Lack of recognition. Not recognizing team and individual contributions makes employees feel undervalued and underappreciated. This is even more problematic in our nonprofit sector, where salaries and benefits can already make it challenging to feel valued.
- Tolerance of bullying, including open criticism and gossip. Bullying can take many forms. It can be your manager purposefully criticizing a mistake you made in a meeting with dozens of other people, or it can be rumors swirling around the office about that mistake. It can even be gossip about what you eat for lunch every day. It goes without saying that bullying in any form undermines psychological safety. Per Part 4, bullying and mistake shaming are not good for a culture where we can feel comfortable innovating and making brave decisions.
- Ambivalence to tardiness. It is incredibly inefficient when people are consistently late to meetings. It wastes time and energy (because sometimes you have to repeat yourself to accommodate latecomers). It also can erode equity, because the group may decide to wait for certain people but carry on without other people. This is counterproductive if you are trying to encourage people to speak up and assure them their contributions are valued.

All these unprofessional behaviors undercut our work from the inside. We will talk about how to address these problems in Chapter 5.3, but first let's talk about what we can learn from the for-profit sector about how we look from the outside.

Branding and Marketing

Branding and marketing. Those words sound so for-profit-y, right? We need to change that.

In today's largely digital world, nonprofits are competing with literally everyone else for supporter attention. We're competing with for-profit companies with huge advertising budgets, and other nonprofit organizations with punchier taglines. We're competing with Kim Kardashian and Donald Trump and the latest social media influencer who is inventing a new makeup technique, getting to the next level in a video game, or kneading dough filled with glitter. People do not consume messages as "this is for-profit" and "this is nonprofit." All incoming information is jumbled together.

We are also getting increasingly impatient in our digital lives: our attention span is now eight seconds long, a decrease from twelve seconds back in 2000 (Microsoft 2022). On their website, Google's marketing team even uses the term "micro-moment" to describe that crucial moment when somebody wants to learn something, do something, go somewhere, or buy something.

Billy Shore, cofounder and chairman of the board for Share Our Strength, broke it down for me like this: "To compete in the real world, organizations are going to have to find ways to make what they're doing accessible and interesting to people. If enough people cared about childhood hunger, we would have solved this problem thirty years ago. But people don't, so we're constantly trying to reach people and persuade them that they should, and we reach a fraction of the people that more entertaining media reaches."

Billy gave me an example of a nonprofit that really understands how to make what it does of interest to a much larger audience. National Geographic uses TV shows, books, magazines, and documentaries to access people well beyond its core audience—those who self-identify as explorers. It is also expert at using visually compelling content that catches people's attention, and its yellow border brand is iconic.

I should mention that in 2015, the Nat Geo magazine, book, map, and other media assets were sold by its nonprofit parent organization to a for-profit venture that's principal shareholder was originally 21st Century Fox and is now Disney. The $725 million payment was intended to allow the organization to double its spending on research, science, and other projects (Farhi, 2015). However, Nat Geo's brand was powerfully recognizable well before 2015 when Disney brought over its marketing machine. For instance, that arresting "Afghan Girl" cover was in 1985.

WHAT IS BRANDING AND MARKETING, EXACTLY?

A common misconception is that your brand is your logo, your website, or your vision statement. Actually, brand is another word for reputation. Your brand is how people think and feel about your organization, both consciously and sub-consciously (Brenner and Heyman, 2019). What comes to mind when you see a Starbucks sign? How do you feel when someone tells you they sell stuff on Etsy? What vibe do you get when somebody says "Amtrak"?

According to Peter Economides, a brand strategist who has worked with Apple, Coca-Cola, and Heineken, the most successful brands are authentic, consistent, relevant, and agile. Literally everything about your nonprofit communicates your brand, not just what you do proactively, but also what you don't do, what you say, what you don't say, how you interact with your volunteers, the quality of your T-shirts or other giveaways, or things that happen related to your brand. The public will determine your brand—just ask Spirit Airlines, Chick-fil-A, or Walmart.

Marketing is building awareness of your organization and brand, ideally to the largest audience possible to reach the largest number of potential supporters. If people don't understand you, how your organization is different, and why you're important, they have no reason to support your work (Brenner and Heyman, 2019).

When you know that your brand is essentially how people feel about your organization, you realize that branding and marketing does not happen overnight. The process can take many years. For example, as anyone who has been on the receiving end of their marketing campaign knows, AARP does not wait until you are membership age (fifty) to start soliciting you.

Having a strong brand can earn you several key benefits:

1. Minimize competitive threats. Your supporters have choices, and you rise to the top.
2. Prepare you for strong partnerships. Clarity about what makes you special and unique makes it much easier for you to effectively coexist with others in your field. (We covered this more fully in Part 4.)
3. Defend against negative news. A resilient brand like Coca-Cola took a hit with "new Coke" but remained strong, compared to Uber and Peloton's continuing struggles.
4. Enhance your supporters' self-image. When associating with your brand makes them feel good about themselves, your supporters will proudly promote you to their own networks.
5. Make better strategic decisions. Using your authentic brand as a lens helps you make better decisions about what to do and what not to do (Brenner and Heyman, 2019).

CORPORATE MARKETING

Corporate marketing in the for-profit sector is a huge machine. Armies of marketers, including those who specialize in brand marketing, advertising, content marketing, event marketing, video marketing, social media marketing, search engine optimization, and more, spend billions of dollars making sure their target audiences see and hear about their brands and products (Financesonline 2022).

Paid advertising is only a subset of total marketing spending, but ad spending in the US across all markets in 2021 includes staggering numbers. Companies spent $157 billion for digital, $70.6 billion for TV, $63.5 billion for mobile, and $10 billion for radio advertising (Statistica 2021). On average, marketing is 11 percent of company budgets, but varies from 4 percent in the energy industry (due to low competition) to 24 percent in consumer packaged goods (WSJ 2017).

All this money and focus on marketing is an ongoing challenge. "With the possible exception of information technology, we can't think of another discipline that has evolved so quickly. Tools and strategies that were cutting edge just a few years ago are fast becoming obsolete, and new approaches are appearing every day," said marketing experts Marc de Swaan Arons, Frank van den Driest, and Keith Weed in a 2014 *Harvard Business Review* article.

The steady rise of competition—from each other, the social media influencers of the world, and some of us nonprofits—means that for-profit businesses are not going to back away from marketing anytime soon.

WHY NONPROFITS LAG BEHIND ON BRANDING AND MARKETING

Many nonprofit leaders believe talking about branding and marketing is tacky. Often these terms are associated with "selling something," and sometimes these terms even connote manipulation or coercion to get people to buy or support things they do not want or need. However, having a good reputation where people trust you and support what you're doing is not trickery. Doing great work and helping people in big ways is not sufficient if nobody knows you exist. Your organization is not going to be sustainable if potential supporters cannot learn about you, engage with what you do, and offer you their skills or money.

Erica Parker is managing director at The Harris Poll, a research-based consultancy. She helps both for-profits and nonprofits evaluate and build their brands. Nonprofits that seek The Harris Poll's assistance recognize they need to think more like a consumer brand and build their brand more like a for-profit would. Many of Harris's nonprofit clients want to get a baseline understanding of their brand and the competitive landscape. Some also contract for qualitative research, where Harris talks to current and prospective donors to get a deeper understanding of the brand.

"Nonprofit missions can be very complicated, and they don't always translate," said Parker. "An organization may think it's really clear on what its mission is, but our work together can help its staff realize it's a little too technical, or a little too internally focused, or that something needs to be simplified."

One of the challenges with nonprofit branding and marketing can be the experience level and sophistication of nonprofit communications staff, which could also be related to the stigma about "selling." Parker also finds that sometimes her nonprofit clients are less prepared organizationally than her for-profit clients. "I do feel like nonprofits have historically prioritized areas other than marketing and are now trying to catch up. For example, they lack the level of integration across marketing channels that for-profits recognized the value of about ten years ago," she remarked.

Another challenge in the nonprofit sector is the belief that branding and marketing have to be expensive. John Vranas, a veteran nonprofit marketing executive, told me, "Branding themselves is the biggest thing nonprofits can do, and probably the cheapest." (More details to come in the very next chapter.)

Sometimes in nonprofits, marketing gets conflated with fundraising. In for-profit businesses, marketing and sales (sales for for-profits is equivalent to fundraising for nonprofits) are two processes that are largely independent of each other. Marketing is building awareness of your brand to potential customers. Sales is identifying the most promising potential customers and converting them into actual paying customers. In both cases, selling/fundraising is not the only outcome of marketing.

Combining marketing and fundraising functions is a trend in the nonprofit sector, and nonprofit leaders have varying views on whether that is a positive direction. Regardless of how the two functions are structured organizationally, marketing experts agree they need to be carefully coordinated.

Katrina VanHuss, CEO of Turnkey Consulting, helps nonprofits with fundraising strategy. She is seeing how new technologies are making marketing and fundraising functions more intertwined. "More and more, marketing tools are used for nurturing development and not just their more traditional use of softening the ground. Facebook fundraising is a great example: this tool that marketing departments were using for building awareness is now raising revenue," she said. "The marketing folks want to keep control of Facebook, but the fundraisers want to take it over."

Marketing typically focuses on "us" (the product, the organization), while fundraising must focus on "them" (the customer, the donor). Just like good sales focuses on the customer ("This shirt/coffee/mortgage will make you smarter/sexier/more envied by your friends"), good fundraising focuses on the donor. "Fundraising helps an individual accomplish their personal goals and achieve their personal satisfaction through the association with the organization," said VanHuss.

Many nonprofit organizations extend their marketing language into fundraising. "The knee-jerk response to 'write me some fundraising copy' is to write things like, 'Help us cure X,' or 'With your dollars we can do Y.' Instead, great fundraising copy has a focus on the donor like, 'You can cure X by doing this,' or 'We know you are angry about Y; here's what you can do about it.'"

VanHuss gave me an example of how "sales" thinking in nonprofit fundraising works better. "We helped one small nonprofit with their year-end fundraising campaign. Previously, it ran undifferentiated campaigns for the most part. Everything was a blend of marketing and fundraising… lots of awareness building with soft asks mixed in. We redesigned the fundraising campaign to focus on what was in it for their donors. Their year-end campaign went from under fifty thousand dollars to two hundred thousand year over year," she concluded.

The problem with differentiation between marketing and fundraising for many nonprofits is exacerbated by the fact that their performance objectives are distinct. Parker of The Harris Poll sees this challenge. "Sometimes, the incentives are in the wrong places. Their key goal is to raise donations, so putting an investment in more top-of-the-funnel brand building can be difficult because they do not see an immediate ROI," she told me.

Many years ago, when I was a junior staffer at AARP, the organization paid a stunning amount of money to an advertising agency for a new logo and tagline. To me and my other junior level friends—none of us marketers—the joke was that "we paid a zillion dollars for them to change the color, un-italicize the R and the P, and remove one of the underlines?" We did not appreciate the massive marketing machine we were up against as a nonprofit.

How do we get smart and strategic about branding and marketing when we don't have zillions of dollars to spend? Let's discuss accountability and inexpensive ways to promote our work.

How to Borrow from Business

How to Borrow from Business:

1. Increase accountability
2. Use best practices for branding and marketing

INCREASE ACCOUNTABILITY

Highly professional for-profit corporate cultures are disciplined and consistent in designing and enforcing their cultural norms. Professionalism is essentially about adherence to a defined set of standards, so your first step is to set clear standards and expectations. Your standards and expectations should encourage respect, which in a professional sense includes the language and approach for interacting with others in the workplace.

Be disciplined in communicating what is expected or permitted in the workplace. Your organization should have a handbook (likely virtual these days) that clearly states the rules for things like respectful interaction, communication formats, communication response times, office relationships, and conflict resolution. The handbook should also clearly and explicitly define the consequences for violations. You should find ways to ensure all staff members read and understand the handbook. Ideally, you should also include your professionalism standards on your formal performance evaluations.

You can offset any tendency to drift toward unhealthy "family" comparisons by creating organizational values and adhering to them. For example, at KABOOM! we had five traits which were essentially our values: "Can do," "Will do," "Team fit," "Damn quick," and "Damn smart." We tied everything to those traits, from hiring to recognition to annual performance reviews, and the terms were part of our shared vernacular.

As leaders, we need to actively encourage professionalism and not just assume that our staff members will automatically acquire it. This leads us to accountability. Generally speaking, most people who work in nonprofits want to contribute to the mission and do good work. Therefore, accountability should not be about mandating compliance, but about creating an environment where staff members voluntarily display commitment and self-discipline (Pennington, 2015).

According to author and former nonprofit executive Randy Pennington, three things you can do right now to build a culture of accountability are:

- Adjust your mindset. Staff members show up on their first day at work wanting to take ownership and succeed. Only about 2–5 percent of your staff members don't want to do a good job, so stop thinking of the other 95–98 percent as the problem.
- Make sure you are doing your part. As a leader, be honest with yourself on areas where you are not fulfilling your responsibility and plan to improve.
- Focus relentlessly on relationships. The difference between mandated compliance and volunteered commitment can often be traced to the quality of the relationship between the leader and follower. People will do what they are told to do because it is their job. As we discussed in Part 3, they will jump through hoops to succeed for a leader they trust and admire (Pennington, 2015).

To curb a tolerance of poor performance, experts suggest that you define what "high performance" means in your organization and publicize it. It can be helpful to identify performance behaviors that "meet" and "exceed" expectations. Ideally, these definitions and standards would be included in your annual employee evaluations (Eagle Hill 2015).

Experts also recommend you identify your high performers and focus your efforts on retention. I have participated in these sorts of efforts before and realize it can feel uncomfortable. However, if you have defined and publicized "high performance" and are tracking all employees against those standards, nobody can claim ignorance about what it takes to succeed in your organization (Eagle Hill 2015).

Per the team-building activities that are so prevalent in our nonprofit culture, you can use them in more productive ways. If you are responsible for planning group activities, make them relevant to the work. For example, if your team is challenged by everyone contributing equally, do something that reinforces that skill. Something like playing paintball seems less relevant to team learning about equal contribution than playing a game where everyone must contribute for the team to succeed.

On the other side, if you are forced to participate, ask questions of the leaders. Try to—verbally, publicly—tie the activity back to team and organizational goals, even if the leaders cannot. If you must play paintball, perhaps you can suggest special rules that are more focused on team collaboration than individual contributions. Make sure to drive home the lessons learned after the team-building games are over. Ask, "What did we learn?" or "How can we apply this to our professional responsibilities?"

A WORD ABOUT INTERNAL COMMUNICATIONS

In my experience leading large-scale organization-wide processes, nothing can be accomplished within an organization without frequent, clear, intentional internal communications.

Internal communications (IC) means keeping staff connected and informed and creating a shared understanding of culture, strategy, and goals. Your staff need to feel connected to your organization, including decisions, initiatives, programs, changes, and what you are sharing externally. When staff feel informed and understand what drives decisions and changes, they are more likely to be receptive and engaged. Strong IC propels and sustains change.

If staff feel disconnected from what is going on and do not understand why decisions are being made, many things are at risk, including morale, retention, mixed messaging to external stakeholders, and both individual and organizational performance.

Recognizing that IC is not a one-way street is also important. You should also have mechanisms for staff to ask questions, air concerns, and provide input. Hearing about what is happening on the ground can be very valuable for management. One of my coaching clients set up a "suggestion box" email address that anonymizes incoming emails to allow employees to ask questions, register complaints, and report violations of the employee handbook.

To engage staff effectively, IC needs to reach them on their terms. You need to consider what they need to know, when they need to know it, and how they want to receive the information. This means that—like any other program—your IC function needs goals, strategies, and metrics.

- Set goals. You want to be intentional about engaging staff with IC. How often do you need to communicate things like big decisions, updates, or performance data? Do you need your staff to acknowledge receipt or respond? What kind of discussions or feedback loops are important?
- Develop strategies. Select IC tools that help you reach your goals and track meaningful metrics. A myriad of such tools are available, from old-fashioned ones

(newsletters, all-staff meetings), to more modern ones (mobile apps, push notifications), so do your homework. Don't forget the two-way street; your strategies and tools should provide opportunities for staff to ask questions and share input.

- Track meaningful metrics. Your metrics should track your goals. For example, if your goal is to solicit input on organizational changes, track how many people comment, "like," or start a discussion.

USE BEST PRACTICES FOR BRANDING AND MARKETING

Luckily, documentation of the best practices of for-profit branding and marketing is widely available. Arons, van den Driest, and Weed describe a massive study called Marketing2020 that collected data from hundreds of chief marketing officers and thousands of marketers all over the world. It looked at everything from brand strategy to data analytics capabilities to employee training. The authors identified the best branding and marketing practices of the highest performing companies.

I will summarize those winning practices for you here, along with the opportunities for nonprofits (that don't break the bank!) for each:

1. Big data, deep insights

Companies are collecting reams and reams of customer data. High performing companies can integrate data on what customers are doing with knowledge of why they're doing it. This combination can yield new insights into customers' needs and gives companies the opportunity to find ways to meet those needs.

Companies use data to know exactly what us customers will buy, how many we'll buy, and at what price we'll buy it. Facebook knows that I was looking at backpacks on Amazon. Uber Eats knows what toppings I like on my pizza. Toyota knows that more of us want black cars than red cars. Lately, companies also know what social causes we want them to support (e.g., climate change, curing breast cancer).

This harkens back to Peter Economides's brand principles of relevance and agility. In this age of eight-second attention spans, if you're not relevant, you are replaced in your supporter's heads with something else. It also stands to reason that you cannot stay relevant if you are not agile.

The vast majority of US nonprofits are not currently capable of collecting and analyzing reams and reams of data. In a survey of hundreds of nonprofits, 90 percent of respondents said they sometimes or always tracked data, but 49 percent said they either don't know or weren't sure about the ways their organization was collecting data. Only 40 percent said they use data very often to make decisions, and 46 percent said they do not consistently use data to make decisions (State of Data 2018).

Like we discussed in Part 2 around measuring what matters, collecting data but not using it to influence your decisions is a waste of time. In this large survey, nonprofits indicated that they weren't confident in the effectiveness of utilizing data; only 6 percent of respondents said they felt they were effectively using data, and 33 percent said they weren't using data effectively or at all (State of Data 2018).

While this is bleak, the good news is that 97 percent of the nonprofits surveyed expressed interest in learning how to use data more effectively (State of Data 2018). Also, we are at an unprecedented time in technology. The vast array of technology options out there can expand your network and amplify your voice.

According to this large survey, here are the top factors non-profits said were preventing them from using data and what you can do about them:

- Not enough time or personnel to focus on data. Using data can save you time and money. For instance, data can help streamline your fundraising process. If you track data about supporters and potential supporters, you can eliminate spending time and money on things you know don't engage them.
- Not enough experience using data. Data collection and analytics does not need to be a full-time job. You don't need a new full-time role; you can designate somebody

to be the data gatekeeper and ensure they understand the software well enough to assist others.

- Data are not centralized. Ideally, invest the time and energy to create a central location and the right software for your data.
- Lack of tools to analyze data. A plethora of software tools exist at various price points. Many well-known, name-brand software products have reduced rates for nonprofit organizations. Do your homework, find one that works for your organization, and go for it.
- Not collecting enough data (State of Data 2018). See Part 2 to help figure out what you need to be collecting.

One of my clients, NAMI Montgomery County, Maryland, embarked on a performance data journey after implementing its new strategic plan. The staff was overwhelmed at first about what to measure and how to collect, analyze, and share the data. The road was long and arduous, involving lots of discussion and a new software system. Happily, they have a staff person with the right skill set who took charge of collecting and analyzing the data.

The organization discovered some interesting things. For example, the demographics of its program participants did not match the county demographics as well as the staff had hoped. Mental illness is a challenge in all parts of the community, and some of the organization's funders prioritize matching these demographics. Having the data armed staff with the information they needed to do more targeted outreach to certain parts of their community and continue tracking the numbers to see if those efforts are successful.

2. Purposeful positioning

The most successful companies create a powerful and clear brand purpose and focus on all three parts: (a) functional benefits, (b) emotional benefits, and (c) societal benefits.

Nonprofits *are* purpose organizations, so we do societal benefits pretty well. We are typically skilled at appealing to supporters' emotions, often using heartbreaking or inspiring messages that connect with people's human core. We love a good story, and we often put the individuals with the lived experience in front of the cause, including victims and survivors.

In his famous TED talk and corresponding book, Simon Sinek explains his concept of "Start with Why." An organization's "why" is what motivates people—and there just may be some science here. Sinek's theory is that successfully communicating your "why" connects with the listener's limbic brain, which is the part of the brain that deals with feelings and not logic. Your "why" can inspire feelings of trust and loyalty, as well as differentiate your brand from others.

St. Jude Children's Research Hospital is consistently the gold standard in nonprofit branding. The Harris Poll EquiTrend Equity Score is an annual brand equity study that compares the brand health of more than 1,700 brands across two hundred categories—including airlines, auto manufacturers, hotels, financial services, and nonprofits. (Its ratings for nonprofits are based on "likelihood to donate time or money.") In 2021, St. Jude was named Health Nonprofit Brand of the Year, as well as the Most Trusted Brand and the Most Loved

Brand among health nonprofits. It has been on the top of several of these lists for many years.

John Vranas spent almost twenty years at St. Jude, culminating as its senior vice president leading development, communications, and marketing. He spoke highly of the organization's brand discipline. "The backbone of its brand is that no child who ever comes here is ever going to pay. It keeps its brand very, very clear," he said.

Contrary to what a lot of nonprofit leaders believe, good branding doesn't have to break the bank. Sure, you could hire a fancy agency to develop your logo (like AARP did) or buy a Super Bowl ad, but creating a powerful brand doesn't require a huge budget. Being disciplined and streamlined about your brand messaging is free (or could even be a cost saver). Creating social media accounts is free. You could use free or low-cost services, software, and programs like Photoshop, Canva, Hootsuite, and Mailchimp to create and share slick branded content. Earned media is, by definition, earned instead of purchased.

3. Total experience

High performing companies add to the value of their products by creating customer experiences. Examples include personalization and an increased number of touchpoints.

With the amount of data we can collect and analyze about current and potential supporters and donors, we nonprofits could do more to deliver a total experience. However, many of us cite shortages of resources and personnel for only focusing on key individuals like sponsors and major donors for this kind of attention.

1. Connect marketing to the business strategy and the rest of the organization

High performing companies realize that marketing is too important to be left just to the marketers. All employees in the company must understand its marketing mission. The most successful companies ensure this happens by creating marketing goals that support company goals and bridging organizational silos by integrating marketing with other departments.

In our sector, it is particularly critical that our fundraisers fully understand and experience our organization's mission. The more immersed they are in the impacts the organization is having or trying to have, the better equipped they are to do their jobs. "I talk with so many organizations where the fundraisers don't get to see what's going on on the mission side. How do they know what they're fighting for when they're out there asking for money?" Vranas wondered.

This connection is something St. Jude does very well. Vranas described the association that St. Jude employees feel to the mission, "At St. Jude, the mission is inherent from the first time an employee sets foot on that campus. You can see that what you're doing makes a difference when you meet the kids and meet the doctors," he said.

Finding ways to ensure that all your staff are connected to your mission is likely an inexpensive undertaking.

2. Inspire

High performing companies engage not only customers but also their employees with their brand purpose. These businesses get everyone excited about and proud of the brand.

At KABOOM!, we encouraged all staff to participate in a playground build in their first few months at the organization. At NAMI, all staff were encouraged to get trained in answering helpline calls and to spend a few shifts doing so. Both these practices ensured that all of us—whether we were an accountant or a strategic planner or a front desk receptionist—could connect to the core of how each organization helps people. It didn't cost us anything but a few hours of a staff person's time, but the glow each of us felt after having these experiences was priceless.

3. Focus on a few key priorities

High-performing for-profit companies have clear brand goals and measure them against key performance indicators such as revenue growth. They plan and execute with precision.

St. Jude's discipline is admirable here. "Of the thousands of kids it treats every year, it chooses about ten to twelve stories and then builds those stories into everything that it does," reported Vranas. That much repetition goes against my intuition. I asked him if people get sick of hearing about little Charlie week after week. St. Jude's track record does not lie. "Most charities hit a billion dollars a year and they start to crumble. St. Jude has managed not to do that. It's only gotten better over time," he said.

I would be a lax strategic planner if I didn't take this opportunity to point out that having a clear organizational strategic plan will make choosing your key branding and marketing priorities a lot easier. Also, it doesn't cost anything to create and measure yourself against goals.

4. Organize agile, cross-functional teams

There is no standard, ideal organizational blueprint. However, the Marketing2020 study suggests that successful marketing structures are moving from rigid, complex organizational structures to more flexible networked structures. This fluidity allows for quicker decision making. Some such structures allow leaders to assemble teams for specific marketing initiatives that are often short-term.

Perhaps this insight could relate to the interplay between the marketing and fundraising functions that we discussed previously. The team-of-teams model mentioned in Part 3 also comes to mind. However the two functions are structured and wherever the various staff sit, marketing decision making needs to be swift.

5. Build internal capabilities.

In this rapidly evolving marketing environment, high performing companies adapt roles and processes. Marketing departments traditionally populated by generalists are flexing to include new specialist roles, in large part due to the importance of social and digital marketing. The most successful companies also prioritize training—some have even set up dedicated marketing academies—to build marketing skills for everyone from the most junior staff to the C-suite.

This ties back to Erica Parker's observation of the relative inexperience of marketing professionals in the nonprofit sector. This seems like it could be a skill set ripe for some of the leadership development suggestions we covered in Part 3, or some cross-sector collaboration where for-profit marketers coach nonprofit marketers.

One nonprofit training example I have seen is staff media training. At AARP, I had to practice delivering talking points with a media person and a camera for about an hour before being allowed to go to outreach events around the country. Unfortunately, this preparation is generally limited to only people with external roles, which means most of the staff may not be aware or bought in to how the organization presents itself to the public.

There may be a cost associated with training or coaching but having savvier marketers to improve your brand and reach more potential supporters is well worth it.

Speaking of training, it's worth noting that the standard training for many for-profit sector professionals, the Master of Business Administration (MBA) is intentionally crafted. In 1959, a report by two national foundations found business school programs were lacking high enough standards and therefore not meeting the needs of American businesses.

The nation's business schools rose to the occasion and transformed their curricula. In 1949, just over 3,000 people graduated with MBAs; today about 150,000 graduate with that degree each year (Callanan, et al, 2014). While some non-profit sector employees have MBAs, it is not a requirement in our sector. We have an opportunity to create a training or widely recognized degree program and make it serve our organizations' needs the way MBA programs serve for-profit businesses' needs.

Borrowing the right tools and practices from for-profit businesses can propel our work forward without compromising our missions. Getting smart about professionalism and branding and marketing can also help bring in more funding. But will all this be enough for our funders?

PART 6

MONEY FOR NOTHING

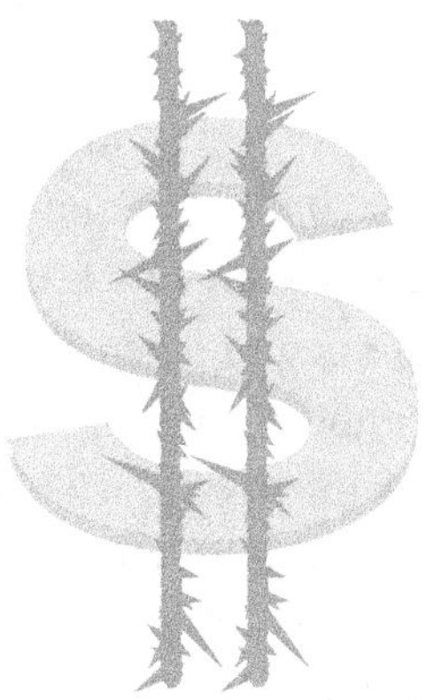

This would not be a bona fide nonprofit management book if I didn't talk about funding. Obviously, the need to raise money is what keeps many of us up at night. They don't call it the "Nonprofit Starvation Cycle" for nothing (Gregory and Howard, 2009).

I want to unpack how we are funded, why it is problematic, and what we can proactively do about it. A few points before we begin:

- I'm not going to tell you how to fundraise. Plenty of books, articles, and consultants can tell you how to do that a lot better than I can.
- I am going to focus on foundation funding here. Do not take this as a snub of fundraising from individuals;

Americans donated more than $410 billion to nonprofits in 2017, and nearly all Americans donate some amount every year (Reich, 2019). However, money from individual donors usually does not come with strings attached the way that so much foundation, government, and corporate funding does. I am focusing on grant funding because that's what's broken.

- Foundations are not a monolithic group. There are approximately one hundred thousand private foundations in the US. Sixty-three percent of them have assets less than $1 million, and 2 percent of them have assets more than $50 million (Foundation Source 2021).
- This section is not intended as a list of gripes. Awareness is half the battle, and each observation I share has corresponding actions that we nonprofit leaders can take to overcome the challenges.
- I will protect the well-meaning by using pseudonyms for my "bad" examples but proudly share the real foundation names in the examples of grantmaking greatness.

In Part 6, we will identify the power of the philanthropic sector. We will examine how the way foundations currently fund us detracts from the four major points I have made in this book: growing impact, building sustainable leadership, making brave decisions, and borrowing what's best from business. We will celebrate some foundations that are working to correct some of these grantmaking frustrations.

Last but not least, we will rally behind what we nonprofits can actually *do* about the foundation situation to ensure we get the funding we need, how we need it, in order to continue our work in solving massive societal problems.

What's Up with Foundations?

Grant funding for nonprofits is broken. What does that look like for us in the trenches? I have my own tales of woe, but I wanted to hear directly from a foundation fundraiser. I spoke with Amse Heck—chief development officer at EveryMind, a Washington, DC, area mental health nonprofit—about her experiences with foundation funding.

"In a nonprofit I worked for previously, we had all the typical foundation funding problems. We were in the cycle of applying for grants and administering new grants and having the courtship periods. Writing the proposals, creating the financials and the logic models, and all the different hoops we have to jump through was a burden that nobody was paying for," she said. "The grants never covered all our administrative costs."

I asked her why the organization applied for so many grants. "We've all been told that if we don't have diversified funding streams, we're not competitive for other grants," she replied. "We have to show sustainability, but how do we show that when many foundations only have a two- to three-year limit on funding one organization?

"To keep our funding 'diversified,' we often extended ourselves into something that didn't quite fit. Once you promise one funder one thing that's not part of your strategic vision, then you're diluting your mission and you're diluting the passion of your staff," she continued.

I asked what that was like for both meeting the mission and staff morale. "We would have to cater to all these different [foundation funder] masters. We kept winning grants and hiring people to run the newly funded programs. By the time we ramped up, the grant was halfway over, and we were going to lose the funds because we couldn't meet the metrics, and then we'd have to fire people, which was very disheartening," she lamented.

Sadly, Heck's experience is far from unique. If you have spent time in and around nonprofits, you have likely heard stories like this. Foundations hold all the power in these asymmetrical relationships.

I can't wait to really dig into the problems foundations cause for us in Chapter 6.2. But first, let's set a little context about the American philanthropic sector.

BACKGROUND ON AMERICAN FOUNDATIONS

America's foundations hold more than $1.2 trillion in assets (Candid 2020). In 2021, foundations gave $88.6 billion to tens of thousands of nonprofits. For context, giving by corporations was only $16.9 billion the same year (Giving USA 2021). Researchers at Boston College predict that rich individuals—led by aging baby boomers—will transfer additional trillions of dollars to foundations and charities over the next few decades (Meehan and Jonker, 2019). With this anticipated influx of money to foundations over the next twenty to thirty years, foundations will play an even more important financial role for nonprofits in the future.

Briefly, most American foundations are private foundations, where the funding typically comes from a single individual, family, or corporation that makes grants to nonprofits. There are also community foundations, which facilitate and pool donations from individuals, families, businesses, and government grants to support local nonprofits. (There is also something called an operating foundation, but they don't give grants, so we won't include them here.)

In his scathing critique of philanthropy, *Decolonizing Wealth: Indigenous Wisdom to Heal Divides and Restore Balance*, philanthropy insider Edgar Villanueva wrote: "The field of philanthropy is a living anachronism. It is like a stodgy relative wearing clothes that will never come back in fashion. It is adamant that it knows best, holding tight the purse strings. It is stubborn. It fails to get with the times, frustrating the younger folks. It does not care."

He means that the nature of foundation grantmaking largely reflects the priorities and whims of foundations, not the needs of nonprofits or the communities they help. Many foundations continue policies, practices, and priorities established a long time ago. Some are opaque, labyrinthine bureaucracies that struggle to be nimble or responsive to community and nonprofit grantee needs. Others are tiny with few or no staff yet are equally mysterious in how they prioritize perceived community needs.

Since the events of 2020, there has been a lot of chatter about transforming grantmaking. More on that in a minute, but spoiler alert: We still have a long way to go.

POWER

Foundations wield an enormous amount of power. Obviously, they have vast amounts of wealth, and there is power in holding the purse strings, but it is more than that. They also wield power because they have few pressures on them.

Foundations do not have shareholders, just boards who are associated with the source(s) of money. Foundations are not subject to market forces; they do not have to make customers happy or adjust what they do based on sales and public relations. Foundation staff leaders and board members are not elected by the people, for the people, but instead from within their own networks and ranks. The result is that foundations have more latitude than most other institutions to decide what—and what not—to share with the public.

Nonprofits and convening organizations of nonprofits and foundations have been seeking more transparency from foundations for decades.

Several areas currently lack transparency:

- Transparency about grantmaking policies: Foundations are not required to publish a public agenda of the causes they fund. Furthermore, they can change their minds anytime and without notice to current grantees. They are also not required to have an open application process. As of 2017, 80 percent of foundations did not accept unsolicited proposals (Eisenberg, 2017).
- Transparency about results and outcomes of grants: Foundations are not required to disclose any of the data they collect from grantees about what their grant money accomplished. This robs the nonprofit sector of important information about what programs and interventions are most effective for solving social problems. It also prevents foundations from learning from one another.
- Transparency about investments: Basically, foundations are not required to disclose where they invest their money. They are only required to report the fair market value of

their assets and list their holdings by asset class. The IRS technically requires "additional detail," but foundations interpret that in various ways. Some foundations reveal exactly how many shares of which stocks they own, while other foundations do not reveal anything beyond the market values (Foundation Advocate 2022). This means that, for example, a climate change nonprofit could be funded by a foundation who is heavily invested in fossil fuels and not even know it.

FOUNDATION FINANCIALS

Foundations' wealth is housed on two sides: an investment side and a giving side. The investment side is generally like any private investment fund, designed for the highest return for the most comfortable amount of risk. By law, foundations are required to distribute at least 5 percent of their net assets annually.

Many foundations are designed to exist in perpetuity—literally forever. "Perpetuity" is used in many private foundations' articles of incorporation or bylaws. In 2018, twenty-seven of the largest fifty US foundations were incorporated in perpetuity (Milway and Galligan, 2020). This means that these foundations plan to give away only small percentages of their assets each year so they can continue to do this forever.

Most large foundations have kept their distribution rates close to the minimum 5 percent distribution requirement. In a large study of foundations of all sizes in 2009, the largest proportion of foundations by far (46 percent) granted out between 5–5.9 percent (Foundation Source 2010). A more recent study of foundations smaller than $50 million found that the smallest foundations tend to be more generous than larger foundations. Foundations with assets of less than $1 million distributed 19.2 percent of their total asset balances in 2019, nearly four times the percentage required by law. This rate was considerably higher than the mid-sized and large-sized foundations, which distributed 8.9 percent and 6.1 percent of their assets, respectively (Foundation Source 2021).

Unfortunately, foundations are also allowed to include all their staff expenses, trustee fees, public related investments, and other administrative expenses as part of the 5 percent, so many large foundations are actually giving less than 5 percent of their assets in grants to nonprofits (Eisenberg 2004).

Scholar and philanthropy critic Pablo Eisenberg testified before the Senate Finance Committee in 2004 about raising the minimum payout rate. "The most effective means of increasing the amount of money foundations give in grants to nonprofits is to require that administrative costs not be included in the calculation of the minimum pay out. In other words, foundations should give its current minimum pay out of 5 percent—or better yet, 6 percent—in grants only," he said. Congress did not act.

In 2020, there was mounting pressure on Congress to double the mandatory payout for foundations (and also donor-assisted funds, another type of charitable giving organization) to 10 percent. A large coalition of foundation and philanthropic leaders wrote an open letter to Congress arguing that this increase would infuse the nation's nonprofits with $200 billion in additional funding over the following three years (Charity Stimulus 2022). To date, Congress has still not acted.

SOME RECENT POSITIVE DEVELOPMENTS

At the time of publishing in early 2022, noting that the twin crises of the COVID-19 pandemic and racial justice have had some positive effects on certain foundation practices is important.

Approximately 60 percent of respondents to a July 2020 survey of foundations planned to increase giving beyond what was budgeted for 2020, with an average increase of 17 percent (COF 2020). In a separate survey in 2021, 58 percent of private foundations and 67 percent of community foundations actually spent more in 2020. Unfortunately, 38 percent of private foundations and 27 percent of community foundations decreased spending in 2020 (CCSF 2021).

The two crises are also having an influence on the missions supported by foundations. Foundations surveyed planned to direct about a quarter of 2020 giving to COVID-19. Eleven percent of foundation respondents reported that racial equity was newly a key or primary focus of their work (COF 2020).

Foundation respondents' 2020 racial equity spend was 16 percent of giving on average, up from about 10 percent in previous years (COF 2020).

Many sources have reported significantly larger increases in spending on racial equity year over year. However, some watchdogs—including Lori Villarosa, the founder and executive director of the Philanthropic Initiative for Racial Equity—warn that reports of a massive increase in giving is greatly exaggerated. "In fact, these numbers—based largely on institutional pledges made in press releases following last year's worldwide racial-justice protests—were at best inaccurate and, at worst, dangerous," she wrote. "Our analysis identified only $3.4 billion in confirmed grants for racial equity in 2020. That figure is preliminary… but it's a tiny fraction of the vast sums previously reported. Once all the data is in, we suspect the 2020 figure will be higher, but not by an enormous amount."

Even before the events of 2020 there was increasing focus on how foundation investments align with the stated goals of the giving sides of their houses. Some foundation boards are adding values-driven, non-financial goals to their investment policies. For example, developing policies around diversity, equity, and inclusion might mean investments in funds in which women and BIPOC have leadership roles, or funding investments where the underlying business activity benefits women, BIPOC, or low-income communities (Giving Practice 2018).

One example is the Heron Foundation, which developed an innovative idea to put even more of its tremendous wealth to work for the public good. In 2012, Heron pledged to go "all in" by fiscal year 2017. CEO Clara Miller and her leadership team were not satisfied with having only the 5 percent they were distributing each year to be in service to their anti-poverty mission. They pledged to move their entire $270 million endowment into impact investments that align with their mission (Field, 2017). This meant that even the money the foundation was not yet giving in grants was working in support of social causes.

Heron moved assets into things like an impact investment venture capital fund and nonprofits like the Family Independence Initiative, which aims to help low-income families become financially self-sufficient. It reached its goal in December of 2016. Miller hopes the move will serve as a model for other foundations to bring more of its resources to push social change (Field, 2017).

Disappointingly, only about 20 percent of foundations were proposing changes to their investment practices, like mission-related investments or investing through a racial equity lens, as a response to the crises of 2020 (COF 2020).

While some of the aforementioned trends are positive, they may only be temporary. Ensuring that these trends continue could help nonprofits make true impact.

Now it's time for some hard truths. Let's discuss how the opaque and secretive way foundations fund nonprofits detract from nonprofits' ability to do all the wonderful things we've already discussed, like going upstream, building sustainable leadership, making brave decisions, and borrowing what is best from the for-profit sector.

How Foundations Fund Us Detracts From…

How foundations fund us detracts from growing our impact because foundations:

- Skimp on overhead
- Push their own agendas
- Shun advocacy

How foundations fund us detracts from building sustainable leadership because foundations:

- Cater to charisma
- Hamper diversity, equity, and inclusion
- Cling to tired models

> How foundations fund us detracts
> from making brave decisions
> because foundations:
>
> - Rush the timing
> - Slow down innovation
> - Hamstring collaboration
>
> How foundations fund us detracts from
> borrowing only what is relevant from
> business because foundations:
>
> - Force unreasonable evaluations

1. HOW FOUNDATIONS FUND US DETRACTS FROM GROWING OUR IMPACT (PART 2)

In Part 2, we talked about how we needed to focus on growing our impact, not our numbers. We can do that by pushing upstream and developing and implementing a clear strategy.

Funders often push us to grow numbers, not impact, which keeps us downstream. They want to see that we were able to help one hundred people instead of the fifty we helped before they gave us the money. These so-called "vanity metrics" for pretty annual reports keep us in the shallow part of the stream. The recipients of the funding—both nonprofits and the people they help—are reduced to numbers instead of solutions.

Years ago, I worked on developing performance measures for the Corporation for National and Community Service

(CNCS). As a grant-making agency, we unwittingly created a numbers problem for some of our nonprofit grantees. We were only trying to prevent double counting, but grantees were stressed because we asked them to report two different numbers for children tutored and children mentored. The mentoring numbers were typically lower (it's a more time-intensive activity), and the organizations were worried that we would see lower numbers and cut their funding. I am hopeful that we corrected this worry in time because I would hate to think an organization stopped a valuable activity like mentoring kids because they were scared to report "lower, less impressive" numbers.

Wanting to grow numbers can also cause us to chase money, which leads to "mission creep" and confuses our strategy. Most nonprofit management books, publications, and articles—especially the bizsplainy ones—will tell you to diversify your funding streams. I don't disagree in theory. It makes sense that getting most of your funds from a single source makes you vulnerable if that source dries up.

However, I do disagree in practice because I have seen many nonprofits prioritize getting new money over staying true to their mission and strategy. If the new money advances your mission, theory of change, and strategic plan that you had in place before, then great. If it will require you to develop a new program you hadn't already planned or hire an entirely new skill set, it's likely only going to spread you even more thin on your mission.

"Fund seekers are forced to play games, dangling projects that they know have 'sex appeal,' or reflect the trendy buzzword of the moment to entice foundations to fund them. Many foundations simply will not fund an organization's existing work," wrote Villanueva.

One of my consulting clients is a housing agency that also provides wrap-around services (like job training) related to economic stability. During the pandemic, a funder offered them a large sum of money to set up a food bank. While the leadership team lamented the food insecurity problem and was flattered to be given the opportunity, they declined. It would have pulled focus and resources from their housing work, which was another need that was also skyrocketing during the pandemic.

FOUNDATIONS SKIMP ON OVERHEAD

Data shows that organizations that build robust infrastructure are more likely to be successful. However, most nonprofits underspend on overhead, and the consequences are disastrous. A recent analysis of the grant portfolios of the fifteen largest US foundations revealed a correlation between chronic underfunding of project grants and nonprofit financial weakness. More than half of the nonprofits analyzed had markers of financial stress, including budget deficits and fewer than three months of cash on hand (Eckhart-Queenan, Etzel, and Silverman, 2019).

(FYI, I will use "overhead" and "indirect costs" interchangeably here. Technically, "overhead" is administrative costs associated with a project or program. "Indirect costs" is the more expansive term that includes both administrative costs and all the other expenses shared across all aspects of a nonprofit's work. Overhead is the more common term, and the terms are actually pretty vague when it comes to grant reporting because there is no standardization across grant makers. Broadly, in this section I am referring to things like information technology systems, financial systems, fundraising costs, branding and marketing, and staff training.)

Dan Pallotta shone a spotlight on nonprofit overhead with his seminal 2013 TED talk. In his talk, he states that nonprofits are burdened by the expectation that most of the money they raise go to "the cause." He challenges us all to consider the overhead we need to operate our organizations as also part of "the cause." Even before Pallotta's talk, the Nonprofit Overhead Cost Project examined more than 220,000 nonprofit IRS Form 990s and conducted 1,500 in-depth surveys. Ann Goggins Gregory and Don Howard analyzed this study, survey results, and other data in a 2009 article entitled "The Nonprofit Starvation Cycle."

This research pointed to a "starvation cycle" of persistent nonprofit overhead deficit. First, funders have unrealistic expectations about the costs of running a nonprofit. Second, nonprofits feel pressure to conform to these unrealistic expectations. Third, nonprofits both spend too little on overhead *and* underreport their overhead expenditures. This situation feeds the funders' unrealistic expectations, and the cycle continues. "Over time, funders expect grantees to do more and more with less and less—a cycle that slowly starves nonprofits" (Gregory and Howard, 2009).

In 2016, The Bridgespan Group analyzed the financial records of twenty well-known nonprofits and found the group's median indirect-cost rate was 40 percent, well above the standard 15 percent that many foundations provide (and 10 percent most government contracts provide) in their grants. In 2017, Bridgespan replicated that analysis with a subset of grantees from the five largest US foundations (Ford, Hewlett, MacArthur, Open Society, and Packard) and found a similar pattern (Eckhart-Queenan, Etzel, and Silverman, 2019).

For context, for-profit companies have average overhead rates ranging from 13 to 50 percent, depending on the industry. Among service industries, which provide services as do many nonprofits, the overhead rates trend toward the higher end of the range (Gregory and Howard, 2009).

When you consider what it includes, you can see how under-estimating overhead spending negatively impacts our ability to fulfill our missions. How do we deliver the most effective programs when we don't have a good way to collect and eval-uate the data? How will people find us and trust us without reliable branding and marketing efforts (even inexpensive ones, like we talked about in Part 5)? How do we raise money when we short staff our fundraising department? How do funders trust us if our financial systems are not up to par? How do we ensure a strong, sustainable leadership pipeline when we don't offer training or development opportunities?

The holy grail of grant funds—from a nonprofit's perspec-tive—is the general operating support grant. These unre-stricted grants help organizations cover overhead and plan for the future, invest in staff, and ultimately increase their impact.

Unfortunately, these general operating grants remain difficult to obtain. Of the only 58 percent of foundations in a recent study who give any general operating grants at all, most of them give general operating support to less than 25 percent of their grantees (Buteau et al, 2020).

The authors were unable to identify any significant barriers to foundations providing or increasing general operating grants (Buteau et al, 2020). This gets back to foundations funding according to their own whims, which doesn't serve the nonprofit sector or the people we help. Basically, there is no real reason they cannot give more general operating money.

FOUNDATIONS PUSH THEIR OWN AGENDAS

Most foundation funding is still stuck in issue-based silos. For example, a health foundation will only fund health, and an education foundation will only fund education. As we discussed in Part 2 on going upstream and Part 4 on collaboration, complex social problems almost always cross issue areas. Unfortunately, many foundations still make nonprofits shoehorn our work into their funding silos.

Over the past three decades, "strategic philanthropy" has become quite popular. In an influential 1999 *Harvard Business Review* article that introduced the concept, Michael Porter and Mark Kramer urged foundations to become more strategic by focusing on clear goals, conducting thorough research, framing limited hypotheses, and requiring accountability and rigorous evaluations. They believed this would lead to advancing knowledge and creating social value beyond the money of their grants.

However, in 2014 Mark Kramer and two colleagues wrote a follow-up article indicating deficiencies in this model. This group of experts believes that funders must move beyond this rigid strategic philanthropy model if they really want to help solve big social problems.

They wrote, "As we have watched funders and their grantees struggle and often fail to reach their ambitious goals, we have repeatedly felt a nagging suspicion that the conventional tools of strategic philanthropy just don't fit the realities of social change in a complex world" (Kania, Kramer, and Russell, 2014).

The biggest deficiency is that while strategic philanthropy has proven useful in addressing simple problems, it is insufficient for complex societal problems. Big social problems do not lend themselves to simple hypotheses. Outcomes do not usually happen from a linear chain of causation that can be predicted and repeated (Kania, Kramer, and Russell, 2014).

Another consequence of strategic philanthropy is that it shifts agency for change from the nonprofit to the foundation. In this model, a foundation views its nonprofit grantees as contractors for its own strategy instead of supporting each grantee's best understanding of what its community needs (Kania, Kramer, and Russell, 2014). Like Heck said, nonprofits are closest to the needs of the communities in which they work. The foundation funder is further from community and therefore more challenged to understand and address those needs.

One large foundation, let's call them the Glut Foundation, has an atypically large staff. A leader at this foundation told me they conduct strategic philanthropy in part to justify all these staff salaries. It results in a lot of "naval-gazing funding," where academic program officers "create knowledge" in areas where we already largely know what works. This reduces the funds the foundation has available to support nonprofits who are actually doing the work.

FOUNDATIONS SHUN ADVOCACY

Advocacy involves promoting the cause or interests of a group of people. The purpose of advocacy is often systems change: changing policies, laws, or rules at local, state, or national levels. Some people think advocacy is synonymous with lobbying, but advocacy is much more than just lobbying. Advocacy is anything an organization does to shape the public debate, such as doing research, writing op-ed articles, or educating legislators or voters. Alas, 80 percent of the most successful social changes in the world have required changes to government funding, policies, or actions (Bridgespan 2017).

Yet, a tiny percentage of philanthropic money goes to nonprofit organizations for advocacy work. In 2014, foundation grants for policy and advocacy were $2.6 billion, which was only 4 percent of their total grants. Even less goes to advocacy and community organizing nonprofits (Guerriero and Ditkoff, 2018).

In fairness, private foundations do face some limits, like being prohibited from lobbying directly on legislation unless the bill addresses the way foundations operate. They also cannot support candidates for public office. However, they can support nonprofits that lobby as long as the grants are not designated to influence a specific bill, voter-education projects, and regulatory proposals by government agencies.

According to a recent survey of foundations, many foundation leaders are comfortable with "ground level" advocacy, like research to support policy makers, but reluctant to support public polling or media campaigns. They often do not want to be seen as courting controversy by supporting a particular side on an issue or walking too close to violating federal law (Daniels and Parks, 2020). This is puzzling, since as we learned earlier, foundations have few pressures or accountability for their activities.

I should note that the survey found community foundations are less reluctant about advocacy. Thirty percent of community foundation leaders said they gained more donors than they lost because of their policy work (Daniels and Parks, 2020).

I spoke with a local social justice nonprofit who successfully pushed for major reforms in the DC area. The organization had to frame its advocacy work to funders and potential funders as "change work" and "education of decision makers." "We met with one of our funders who had started speaking to policy makers on our behalf, but she was really sensitive and nervous about advocacy," the organization's executive director told me. "She was telling us about her conversations, and our tongues were bleeding because we were biting them so hard not to say, 'Sister, that is advocacy! You're doing it!'"

If advocacy is what is needed to change the policies, laws, and rules that are keeping our big societal problems unsolved, it is frustrating that it's so hard for us to get funded to do that work.

2. HOW FOUNDATIONS FUND US DETRACTS FROM HAVING SUSTAINABLE LEADERSHIP (PART 3)

In Part 3, we talked about how we need to build sustainable leadership instead of worshipping heroes. We can do that by identifying the right leadership skills, intentionally developing those skills in our nonprofit staff and leaders, and ensuring our organizational structures support those leaders. Sadly, foundations don't make any of this easy.

FOUNDATIONS CATER TO CHARISMA

Funders are often enamored with charismatic "hero" leaders. Too often, charismatic leaders get funded on ideas (or personalities) alone, with little or no evidence of how their ideas will work.

In her book *Emergent Strategy: Shaping Change, Changing Worlds*, adrienne maree brown wrote, "The shiny stars are rarely the ones actually getting the work done, or even doing the most exciting thinking in the organization. If you are in the funding world and your primary relationship with those you fund is with the executive director… you may be stricken with charismitis: relational laziness induced by charismatic brilliance."

A senior executive from a founder-led health nonprofit I interviewed said, "A lot of funders are like, 'Please take some money and make this problem go away.' They'd rather write a big fat check than really get in the communities and get in the circumstances and be involved with this horrible, abusive national trend. They put their money on someone who seems like a subject matter expert. They love charismatic leaders."

This senior executive's organization has serious problems. It is not making any progress toward its mission, and staff are dropping like flies. "The staff are confused; don't our funders see that the founder is not trustworthy? We're not hitting any of our marks because of his poor, scattered leadership. Staff are really frustrated that this behavior keeps getting rewarded," the senior executive reported. The nonprofit is not producing results and has no real strategy to do so. Yet funders are still putting money into the organization.

Research shows that having flashy leaders is not the most effective approach to lasting social change; we need collaboration across a number of different people, organizations, and even sectors. Focusing attention and funds on charisma diverts resources away from leaders and organizations who are more collaborative and possess robust teams with the right attributes to make meaningful social change. Furthermore, foundations do not always evaluate organizational capacity to be effective, including leadership bench strength, before they make grant decisions.

Regarding the leadership development we nonprofits so desperately need, only 1 percent of what we get from US foundations each year is for leadership development (Callanan et al, 2014). This dearth, plus foundations' reticence to fund overhead, severely undermines our leadership development.

It also impedes our efforts to keep top talent in our organizations and even our sector.

FOUNDATIONS HAMPER DIVERSITY, EQUITY, AND INCLUSION

As we also discussed in Part 3, effective leaders surround themselves with diverse networks for many compelling reasons. And as we discussed in Part 4, the number of community-driven and collective models happening within our sector is increasing. All this reflects a need to center our work in the communities with the problems we are trying to solve.

We need to address racial and other disparities and shift the power dynamics. However, foundations are not where we typically find great diversity. The composition of foundations remains essentially the same as a century ago: white, wealthy, and highly trained professionals. The vast majority (92 percent) of foundation CEOs are white, and 89 percent of foundation boards are white (Villanueva, 2018).

Given these numbers, it makes sense that far more foundation money goes to colleges and hospitals than to organizations and institutions that help the poorest in our society or have a specific focus on low-income people, BIPOC, LGBTQA, and other marginalized communities (Villanueva, 2018). As we revealed in Chapter 6.1, 16 percent of foundation funding goes specifically to benefitting BIPOC, which is absurd considering 38.4 percent of our population identifies as something other than "white alone" per the US Census (Jones, et al, 2020).

Sadly, in a survey of foundation leaders conducted in mid-2020, only 13 percent of respondents reported an increased commitment to hiring BIPOC, despite the crises of both the pandemic and racial justice (COF 2020).

What is worse, organizations based in disadvantaged communities and led by local leaders often do not qualify for grant funding because foundations say these organizations don't have the data, don't have the track record, are not big enough, or are not scalable (Villanueva, 2018). This "foundation redlining" hurts us all—the BIPOC leaders who cannot access funding to start and run their organizations, and the sector as a whole because it robs us of these leaders' ideas and perspectives on what may solve social problems.

Villanueva's central argument is that what ails philanthropy is colonialism. "Almost without exception funders reinforced the colonial division of us vs. them, haves vs. have nots, and mostly white saviors and white experts vs. *poor, needy, urban, disadvantaged, marginalized, at risk people*, take your pick of euphemisms for people of color," he wrote.

FOUNDATIONS CLING TO TIRED MODELS

Funders claim to want to foster sustainability, growth, and innovation, but they are not always willing to consider new approaches.

Management and strategy consulting became very prominent for for-profit businesses in the eighties and nineties (Lafitte, 2019). Foundations—whose boards generally live in the business world—saw obvious utility in bringing the consulting model to the nonprofits they fund. The benefits of short-term consultants abound, including targeted expertise, on-demand service, low overhead, and no long-term financial commitment.

Foundations love to fund short-term consulting engagements. Many foundations have a go-to cadre of consultants they require, or at least encourage, their grantees to use. As we discussed in Part 3, when a nonprofit has a larger or more complex need—like making significant changes to move upstream toward solving social problems—short-term consultants are not going to cut it.

Funding a term executive (a full-time leadership position with a time-limited contract of six to twenty-four months, like we covered in Part 3) is much more effective in achieving strategy and organizational change outcomes than a short-term external consultant and also strengthens the organization for the future. Foundations *rarely* have the insight to fund such a position.

This lack of support for larger, complex needs puts great strain on nonprofit leadership. Even when a leader or team of leaders can think strategically about how to make maximum impact, the herculean effort it would take to change operations or program delivery models may be too difficult to execute. Having to manage short-term consultants can also be an additional burden during a big change effort.

One of my friends is a fundraiser at a national economic opportunity nonprofit. With foundation funding, her organization hired a big consulting firm to create its new ToC and strategic plan. However, the staff were too busy and the firm too external to be anything but a perennial afterthought. Unfortunately, almost three years later the plan is neither socialized with staff nor implemented. She's never even seen the ToC. Her and her coworkers refer to it as the "[name of consulting firm] plan." As a result, many staff do not see the full picture of the organization and understand why they do what they do.

If the foundation had funded a full-time strategy person—time-limited or not—on the inside to do this work, the organization would likely have a clearer strategy and better staff engagement. It probably also would have cost less since the organization's work would be more targeted right now.

3. HOW FOUNDATIONS FUND US DETRACTS FROM OUR ABILITY TO MAKE BRAVE DECISIONS (PART 4)

In Part 4, we talked about reframing the benefits of risk taking and making brave decisions. We can do that by learning from the scientific method and collaborating more creatively.

FOUNDATIONS RUSH THE TIMING

Like we discussed in Part 2, the societal problems we work on in the nonprofit sector take time and patience. However, only about half of foundation grants are multiyear funding commitments (Buteau et al, 2020). In one study, more than 40 percent of foundations did not provide any multiyear grants, and only 16.3 percent of foundations designate more than 50 percent of their grant money for multiyear funding (Criteria, n.d.).

Many annual grants have the option to renew one or more times, but the administrative hoops we must jump through via mid-term reports, final reports, examinations of financials, etc. eat into our implementation of the actual work and also make us constantly worried about ongoing support.

The authors of an article in *Nonprofit Quarterly* wonder, "So, when the nonprofit sector tackles our most intractable and wicked problems, why does philanthropy expect a short-term win/lose proposition? Today's [societal] problems have taken generations to develop and will not be solved quickly" (Bennett et al, 2021).

Wendy Jackson, managing director for the Kresge Foundation's Detroit Program (more on that effort later), agreed. "I don't know why philanthropy got into this way of thinking that you could do something in three years and be done," she said.

Philanthropy scholar Rob Reich is very critical about how foundations squander their own timelines. "The institutional design of foundations permits them to operate on a different time horizon than the marketplace and the government. Because their endowments are designed to last, foundations can fund higher-risk social policy experiments, and use their resources to identify and address potential social problems decades away or innovations whose success might be apparent only after a longer time horizon. In short, unlike business and [government], foundations can 'go long.'"

Speaking of innovation, finding foundation funding for that can be difficult. Many grant makers shy away from funding experiments and taking "big bets." A recent review of foundation activity found that only a small fraction of grant making qualifies as big bets for social change (Foster et al, 2015).

I believe that philanthropy insider Villanueva has distinct credibility on this topic.

> *"Philanthropy moves at a glacial pace. Epidemics and storms hit, communities go underwater literally and metaphorically, Black and brown children get shot dead or lose their youth inside jail cells, families are separated across continents, women are abused and beaten and raped, all of Rome burns while we fiddle with another survey on strategies, another study on impact.*
>
> *Other sectors feel the heat of competition, not us. We politely nod at the innovations of the business sector. It takes us a half century to implement one of them. We indulge those who say that diversity is important by conducting several decades of analyses, hiring consulting groups with absurd price tags. We publish reports. We create a task force and debate mightily over what to call it."*

There are some great examples of foundations supporting innovation in the past. For instance, forty years ago the Robert Wood Johnson Foundation funded regional pilots that led to the national 911 system (Kasper and Marcoux, 2014). However, most of them currently prefer to fund proven programs that have predictable results. Perhaps because

endowments, by definition, are investment vehicles for con-
serving resources.

Foundations have all the time in the world to support new
ideas and potential solutions, including collaboration.

FOUNDATIONS HAMSTRING COLLABORATION

There has been an increasing focus on foundation support
of nonprofit collaboration in the last few decades. We know
that social change usually requires collaboration, so this
sounds like it could be good news. However, the way many
foundations currently execute their support for nonprofit
collaboration is counterproductive.

One of the most common flaws is when a foundation names
the problem and then forces partners/grantees to work
together on solving it. As I mentioned before, funders are
often a step or two removed from the community and community needs. When nonprofits are not recognized and supported as the experts at what will help the community, the
programs often fail (Easterling, 2019).

Another issue is a disconnect between what types of collaborations foundations fund (or want to fund) versus which
collaborations nonprofits feel will increase their impact.

Foundations like to fund joint programs, where two or
more nonprofits work together to deliver a program over an
extended period. About 75 percent of nonprofits in a comprehensive Bridgespan study said that foundation funders
provided financial support for joint programs most often,

despite nonprofit reports that these collaborations have less impact than more integrated forms like mergers or shared support function collaborations (where two or more organizations share functions like accounting, HR, and IT). Nonprofits believe these more integrated forms offer the greatest new opportunity for important activities like acquiring new capabilities and expanding their reach (Neuhoff et al, 2014).

Another challenge with current foundation funding of collaboration is logistical. Grants often do not cover the full overhead cost of partnering. Collaboration can be time-consuming and create a burden for staff, particularly in small organizations. It also takes time to build relationships—something that can be difficult when you're on the funding clock.

Foundations are trying several collaboration models and sharing various best practices, but they still have a lot of room for improvement in how they support the kind of creative collaboration that can lead to social change. (See some positive examples in the next chapter.)

4. HOW FOUNDATIONS FUND US DETRACTS FROM BORROWING ONLY WHAT'S RELEVANT FROM BUSINESS (PART 5)

In Part 5, we talked about how we should not strive to be exactly like for-profit business, but to borrow what is most relevant to our work. I suggest borrowing professionalism and branding and marketing best practices, but often our funders want much more than that.

"I've seen funders and grantees speak completely different languages," said monitoring and evaluation guru Saunji Fyffe.

Since many funders have money and power, it makes sense that business is the language they understand. This can be a big hurdle for nonprofits. I spoke with several foundation leaders and discovered some really interesting viewpoints.

FOUNDATIONS FORCE UNREASONABLE EVALUATIONS

Particularly within the business-like, data-driven approach of strategic philanthropy, rigorous evaluations have become more common. Many of the nonprofit leaders I interviewed had experiences with funders requiring their grantees to collect certain data without really understanding whether these data make sense or are actually useful. On the other side, some foundation leaders I spoke with admitted they don't even use all the data they collect.

One foundation leader said, "Impact evaluations are sexy. We need to ask the hard question of 'Did it work?' to start weeding out things that don't so you can focus on things that do. However, we try to do too much of this. It should just be done sparingly, when an initiative is good and ready, and when enough time has passed for us to know anything about if it works."

An executive at another foundation put it a little differently. "We don't all have to do a randomized control trial [RCT, which is a regimented and costly evaluation]. We may never do an RCT, and that might be okay if we're still getting good outcomes. We actually can evaluate and learn as we're implementing. You can either spend all your money doing super rigorous evaluation, or you can spend your money learning and iterating and helping people."

Two separate foundation leaders pointed out possible conflicts of interest. "If we're paying for the evaluation, there's automatically a weird dynamic there. We have an incentive to always look like we're winning or doing the right thing," she said. To me, wanting to look like you're "winning" probably does not allow for a lot of experimenting, failing, and learning.

The other leader got even more granular. "The closer you go to a tight measurement strategy where we prescribe outputs and outcomes, the more it's going to circumscribe innovation because it's really just buying outcomes for our board," he warned.

So, I think it's safe to say that not even foundation staff fully understand their own evaluation requirements for their grantees. Funders often also fail to consider the burden of collecting such data, which takes us back to overhead. A frustrating catch-22: nonprofits need money to invest in overhead expenses like data systems to be able to capture outcome data, yet many funders want to see strong outcome data before they grant general operating support that could be used for overhead (Gregory and Howard, 2009).

Clearly, there is a myriad of reasons why the way many big funders fund nonprofits is hamstringing our ability to be our most effective. Is it all bad news? Is the situation hopeless?

Shining the Light

It's not all bad news! What follows are some examples of foundations that are funding nonprofits in ways that support us growing our impact, building sustainable leadership, making brave decisions, and borrowing the most relevant for-profit business practices.

I recognize that most of the following examples are really large foundations. They clearly have the luxury to explore different ways of doing business thanks to their ginormous endowments. However, another way to look at it is, if these heavies can make changes to how they spend their significant resources, it should be relatively easier for smaller foundations to shift their policies and practices.

THE WILLIAM AND FLORA HEWLETT FOUNDATION

The Hewlett Foundation is a $13 billion foundation that is very focused on systems-level change that gives roughly $500 million in grants annually. Sixty to 70 percent of their grants are typically flexible, unrestricted funding, or general operating support.

I spoke with Carla Ganiel, former organizational learning officer at the Hewlett Foundation, about the importance it places on listening to communities. Hewlett commissioned a field scan to learn how foundations are intentionally listening to and incorporating the perspectives of the people and communities who are most affected by the systemic problems the foundation seeks to address. She said,

> *"There's a lot of suspicion—and sometimes rightly so— about a larger organization that might be further removed from a community. If funders are telling nonprofits to be better listeners, we should also be better listeners ourselves and hear from the people who are the closest to the problem. Since we largely focus on systems change, it is harder for us than it is for other funders who are funding direct service kinds of programs. We're still figuring it out."*

I found this a hopeful sign that this particular funder was not trying to push its own agenda on its grantees or communities. I asked Ganiel for an example.

> *"For instance, we fund Western conservation, and so we asked ourselves who we needed to listen to. We fund public opinion research called the 'Conservation in the West' survey [a bipartisan poll that surveys voters' views on issues like conservation of public lands, energy, water, wildlife, wildfire, and other challenges in eight Mountain West states]. It captures the opinions of people who live there and what they want from conservation. We also actively sought input from ranchers, tribal communities, and other community groups when developing our funding strategy because we understood that conservation efforts can't be*

sustainable without broad support from everyone whose lives are affected."

I also spoke with Adam Fong, program officer in Hewlett's Performing Arts program, about a new approach to grant making they piloted during the pandemic.

"The Mellon Foundation did a set of capitalization grants in 2015 that was inspiration for how we structured some new relatively large grants called adaptation grants. Our intention was to help organizations—most of whom were existing grantees—plan for and implement changes in response to challenges introduced or exacerbated by the pandemic. What were the conditions that had changed and would continue to change? How did they believe they needed to adapt in order to better achieve their mission in the long run?

These grants provide support to grantees to develop an adaptation plan, and then they have two or three years with which to spend the money and report back to us on how far they've gotten. The goals that they set out would be medium- to long-term, like five, seven, ten years out. The expectation was not that they would actually achieve these adaptation goals in that time, but that they would make significant progress and learn a lot along the way."

The foundation is not requiring evaluation of each grant on its own. That's typical for Hewlett, which focuses its evaluation to field-level measurement. They are supporting their grantees' own assessments of their situations, including infrastructure and community needs, on a timeline that allows for intentionality. Fong continued describing these adaptation grants.

> *"Because many nonprofit budgets are stretched so thin, the resources to plan for the future are a luxury. These grants allow them to lift their eyes to try to look out to the horizon despite all of the hardships of the moment, understanding that when things resume it will be a new reality and an opportunity for them to put a different type of stake in the ground.*
>
> *This is ongoing work, and the more we acknowledge that ongoing adaptation is required, the better off we'll be. In essence, we as a sector are building on what we observe and what we know can happen, with the faith that if we invest more in it, it can happen more forcefully and reflect our values more fully."*

Hewlett places trust in its grantees and encourages long-term planning. If funders did this more often, Part 6 of the book would have been much shorter.

THE KRESGE FOUNDATION

The Kresge Foundation is a $4.1 billion foundation that concentrates its work in cities to assist high numbers of people in hardship or poverty that gives about $130 million in grants annually.

I spoke with Wendy Jackson, managing director for Kresge's Detroit Program. This program works with a range of partners, including resident leaders, nonprofit organizations, businesses, and state and city governments in the foundation's hometown of Detroit.

> *"Our place-based approach requires us to work on issues at the intersection of people, place, systems, and power. You can't effectively achieve progress unless you're working on those four fronts. That's what makes place-based philanthropy quite unique. This place-based model is a combination of responsive grant making and strategic philanthropy. We are very much focused on systems change and power building. We partner with nonprofits that have deep history and a track record for this work in Detroit."*

It seems the place-based approach supports upstream thinking in very powerful ways. Kresge combines this with long time horizons.

> *"We've had the ability to provide general operating support for a very long time. We have some partners that we've been supporting for decades because they are a critical part of the nonprofit infrastructure in the city. Our strategy is generational because meaningful change takes time, and the traditional philanthropic funding model of three years of support often doesn't work best in the context of place. You're not going to be able to have the breadth of support for the nonprofit sector when you're just doing project grants all the time."*

To be an effective partner over a longer period of time does require some tough choices. That's the trade off in providing core support over a long period of time. We constantly balance our role to catalyze work that will get uptake by other sectors with consistency. We want our nonprofit partners to know they can depend on us.

Kresge also recognizes the importance of working *with* the community instead of doing things *to* the community.

> *"We are intentional about building the power of the non-profit sector to be an effective advocate for issues and people in the community, particularly with city government. We also value opportunities to build trust and partnerships where communities are making the decisions on where the investment goes and how it gets used."*

Jackson explained a recent project in the disinvested district of Livernois-McNichols in northwest Detroit, where Marygrove College closed its undergraduate programs after ninety years. The foundation was a long-time supporter of Marygrove College and invested to help stabilize it, cushion faculty and student transitions, and support its shift to graduate-level education. Kresge then partnered with the college's founders and sponsors to create the Marygrove Conservancy.

After a collaborative process, the conservancy announced a new cradle-to-career educational partnership, including a state-of-the-art early childhood education center, a new K–12 school, and the introduction of an innovative teacher education training modeled after hospital residency programs. This initiative is one of the first of its kind and is backed by $60 million in Kresge support along with other private and philanthropic contributions. This is the largest philanthropic investment in history into a Detroit neighborhood (Detroit 2022).

Jackson is rightfully proud of the effort and the trust Kresge places in its grantees and community partners.

> *"We worked proactively with the college leaders and other partners to transform what could have been a very devastating story into a new way of thinking about education in the city. We started in a quarterbacking role until others were able to stand up the organization that can now move it forward."*

She also sees that there is significant risk involved.

> *"Place-based philanthropy requires patience and a higher-risk tolerance. You need to be willing to try new things and explore new ideas that are going to push the boundaries for how to build on the assets of a community. Some call it risk. I just call it doing the right thing."*

If only more of us could think about risk taking this way.

THE ANNIE E. CASEY FOUNDATION

The Annie E. Casey Foundation (Casey) is a $3.8 billion foundation that focuses on creating a brighter future for children and young people by using evidence-based approaches to help decision makers remove barriers to opportunity and prevent disconnection from family and communities. Casey gives $118 million in grants each year, 25 percent of which are general operating support.

Casey spends a significant portion of its grantmaking on systems reform. I spoke with John Kim, chief administrative officer at Casey, about that work.

> *"In philanthropy, we are able to think through a challenge, construct a theory of change, conduct research to prove or disprove our theory, identify the problem, and then develop solutions that government and other leaders can take to scale and improve well-being for large populations. We believe heavily in system reform, and it's something that we do well. You have to get to the root of the problem to figure out how to really make lasting change. This is an important role for philanthropy because foundations can take more risks in thinking about systemic changes."*

Whenever anyone talks about the root of a problem, you know they are thinking upstream. One specific example of Casey's upstream work is what they call their "deep-end" juvenile justice reform. The foundation funds and supports communities to enact a range of policies and practices to safely reduce out-of-home placements and address persistent racial and ethnic disparities within the system.

> *"It's pretty common knowledge that institutionalizing children is a bad thing. It doesn't work. There is a lot of pressure on state governments—economic, political, etc.—but the effects on kids are really bad. So how do you change the system? Can you divert some of that money to diversion strategies so that you don't have to confine kids in institutions, or do you redesign institutions? We've played a role in changing that on the ground because governments get stuck in keeping the trains moving. There's no space,*

there's no time, there's too few resources for them to have a different vision."

Kim elaborated on the work.

"It is a very different kind of grant making strategy. We have subject matter experts in teams that can go in and do these things, and we also draw on the help of local grantees. It's a combination of grant making and technical assistance and influence. Governments invite us because we're a private philanthropy that has no political affiliation."

Like Kim says, this is not traditional grantmaking. In addition to funding, Casey staff provide individualized guidance and technical assistance, promote communication and collaboration (including facilitating calls with site coordinators and convening stakeholders from each site), develop tools and resources (for example, a system-assessment process), and collect and review site data. According to its evaluation report for work in 2013–2018, "the foundation sought to define a clear yet flexible deep-end reform approach for sites, tailor that approach to each site, and build sustainable site capacity for reform."

This is actually taking strategic philanthropy to the next level. In the Casey model, in addition to strategic vision, the funder also brings staff expertise and key government relationships to the issue. They also shoulder the responsibility of evaluation. It is heavy-handed yet highly supportive of nonprofit partners because there is much less burden on staff to coordinate partnerships and evaluate program progress.

The changes that Casey helped catalyze around juvenile justice in Virginia are impressive. Virginia's juvenile correctional centers are being downsized. The Department of Juvenile Justice recently awarded contracts for community-based services because youth do better and communities stay safer when high-quality interventions are in their home communities. The state is safely reducing its population of youth in state custody and is heavily investing in staff training and support to improve conditions and culture within the correctional centers (Virginia 2022).

"I can see the trajectory from our involvement, from identifying the root cause of barriers to getting the results kids need," Kim concluded.

ACT FOR ALEXANDRIA

ACT for Alexandria is a community foundation in Alexandria, Virginia, just outside Washington, DC. Founded in 2002, ACT connects donors with causes they are passionate about and collaborates with nonprofits to optimize resources and impact. It awarded $8.6 million in grants in 2020, most of which was general operating and capacity-building support.

I spoke with Heather Peeler, president and CEO of ACT, about her organization's approach to community engagement and racial equity. Peeler came to ACT in 2018 after six years as vice president at Grantmakers for Effective Organizations.

Peeler is very intentional about ACT's structure in how it represents community.

"At first I thought, 'Me and the staff need to be in the community.' But that's not sufficient, we're not of the community. For example, I'm not a recent immigrant from Central America. It would be really presumptuous of me to think that I could represent all the different community member experiences. It doesn't mean that we don't show up and we don't try to get embedded in the community, it just means that we actually never can be of the community."

One way ACT is getting closer to community and being more inclusive is by expanding the size and composition of its board.

"As a community organization, it's about creating more seats at the table. Rather than a 'scarcity mode' of limited seats where you have to be really choosy, we have more of an 'abundance mode' where we can think about all of the strengths and assets and talents that we want to bring into the organization."

ACT's structure has grown under Peeler's leadership, managing the massive disbursement of emergency state and federal government funds on behalf of the city during the pandemic and spearheading several key initiatives around longstanding needs in the community. One of these needs is racial equity.

Alexandria has a complicated history with race relations. The city used to be one of the biggest trafficking ports of enslaved people, and many in the Black community are descendants of people enslaved by George Washington's estates. Alexandria was segregated long after segregation was illegal. For example, it took twenty years after Brown v. Board of Education for the city to have a full integration plan. The 2000 film *Remember the Titans*, starring Denzel Washington, is about the integration of Alexandria City High School's (formerly T.C. Williams High School) football team (ACPS 2022).

The city today is still quite fragmented, despite its liberal politics. ACT has become a key community quarterback in addressing racial equity. In 2019, ACT adopted an explicit commitment around racial equity. It vowed to use its power and influence in service to community members who have been marginalized and discriminated against because of their race and to invest resources in community leaders and in programs and ideas prioritized by people most impacted by systemic racism.

"We're bringing people together and creating space for collaboration and for alignment and using our voice to amplify the voice of others, but also to mobilize people around things that we think are important," said Peeler.

A prime example was ACT's design of a 2019 conference for nonprofits in Alexandria.

> *"In 2019, we hosted a nonprofit conference with the theme of racial equity. Instead of doing a traditional closing plenary, we asked the attendees to tell us what they needed in order to continue that conversation and commitment to racial equity. We then started implementing what they told us. They wanted more training, so we forged a partnership with a training partner and now have trained more than three hundred people. They wanted capacity building support, so*

we made capacity building grants focused on racial equity. We keep evolving that."

This funder is directly addressing diversity, equity, and inclusion—something that many foundations avoid—and it is doing so with deep community engagement.

Let's Wag the Dog

"We need to confront the largely unaccountable, nontranspar-ent, donor-directed, tax-advantaged, and—by default—per-petual power of big philanthropy."

—ROB REICH

Our nonprofit sector can "wag the dog" of philanthropy. Neither government nor the American public are holding foundations accountable for society's intractable problems that these institutions are giving billions of dollars to help solve. Foundations' own boards are also ill-equipped to do so. It has to be our sector.

"We need to inject a dose of courage into our individual and collective spines. We require a growing number of organizations and leaders who will show us that candor and courage, as well as thoughtful approaches, are the avenues to change," said philanthropy critic Pablo Eisenberg.

Amse Heck of EveryMind has been exercising candor and courage. "At EveryMind, we have the benefit of being able to collaborate more with funders because we are somewhat of a local name brand. We're the experts in this community. We know what the people need, and we're the boots on the ground meeting that need. The funders do not always have that connection," she explained. "When I develop relationships with new funders, I explain what we do. I am clear that I hope they see our vision and want to come along."

I asked her how she can be so brave. "We have a strategic plan that we really stick to," she said. "Also, my philosophy as the revenue person is that I don't want to set us up for failure. I don't want to promise something to a funder that we don't have the infrastructure to deliver. I don't want to ever tell a funder that what we promised is outside what we do and so we were not as successful."

When I inquired if Heck had ever turned down funding, she had a recent example. "There is a pretty large foundation in this region that focuses on [another issue tangentially related to mental health]. They're starting to move into mental health and were very interested in working with us. Unfortunately, the funder really felt that it was important to include its own program, which is really outside of our scope. Not that it's not valuable and wonderful, but it's not what we do. And we are lucky to have other funders at that level that fund us for exactly what we do."

I asked her if that was the end of the conversation with that particular foundation. "This is an instance of 'Let's keep the conversation going.' It's been almost two years that we've kept the conversation going, but we just haven't found alignment.

It kind of hurts to not go after the funding, but saying no is keeping us on mission."

Her experience proves that we can speak truth to power. Eisenberg has more advice:

> *"One of the reasons foundations have frequently failed to meet the needs of nonprofits is the accommodating attitude of grantees. Acting like beggars in the philanthropic process, [nonprofit] grantees have been unwilling to assert their views and challenge foundation assumptions and practices... Unless they are willing to change their approach, both individually and collectively, [nonprofit] grantees will continue to be the handmaidens, not the partners, of philanthropic institutions."*

So, let's stop being handmaidens.

THE WAY FORWARD FOR INDIVIDUAL NONPROFIT ORGANIZATIONS

As nonprofit leaders representing our own organizations, we can use our individual voices.

SEEK CULTURE ALIGNMENT

Many nonprofits put themselves at the mercy of funders who have money to give. However, accepting funding that either anchors us in our downstream place without the ability to innovate, or pushes us off course, will ultimately delay—or even prevent altogether—the achievement of our strategies and mission. This hurts nonprofits *and* the people we aim to help.

However, we can find funders with whom our culture aligns. We can find funders—large and small—that support what we're doing if we're patient, we communicate clearly, and we make them believe our "why."

Saying no takes a lot of courage, but we must if we are truly committed to solving big social problems.

COMMUNICATE AND PUSH BACK

Many foundations have not changed their business practices much in decades or even centuries, but maybe part of that is because nonprofits are not brave enough to tell them what we need to be successful. We may not believe that funders would welcome more dialogue with us. We are scared that funding will be denied or withdrawn if we are honest about costs and capacity or if we push back on what feels like unreasonable expectations.

However, if more nonprofit organizations were completely honest with funders, foundations' expectations would have to change. Gregory and Howard of the "Nonprofit Starvation Cycle" believe this. "Our research suggests that taking action at the first stage—funders' unrealistic expectations—could be the best way to slow or even stop the cycle."

We must speak truth to power to break this cycle. A first step might be to treat funders and potential funders as partners instead of the great and powerful Oz. We can do our best to reframe these relationships to ones where we are valued for our expertise and experience about community needs and what can work to solve social problems.

We can signal what is important with the language we use. As we discussed in Chapter 6.2, many funders try to reduce our work to numbers and costs. We can do our best to shift that conversation to outcomes. When a funder wants to know about efficiency or ROI or other mathematical formulations, we can refocus them on how we define success and what impacts we are trying to see in communities. As Gregory and Howard said, "Even focusing on approximate or crude indicators is better than looking at cost efficiencies."

The good news is that, according to several of the foundation leaders I interviewed, foundation staff are much more open to conversation than many of us believe. "There is a lot of baggage associated with monitoring and evaluation because many funders historically used them as tools to 'hold grantees accountable.' As a result, some grantees freak out—justifiably so—when we ask them to have a conversation," said Ganiel of the Hewlett Foundation. "Often, we just want to listen and learn about what progress looks like from the grantee's perspective. We want our grantees to be able to say to us, 'Your expectations for us are unrealistic. What you think we can do in two years, maybe we could do that in five years,' or 'We don't have the capacity to do all of those things,'" she said. "Then we can develop shared expectations that are realistic and grounded in the grantees' expertise, and we can help them build the capacity they need."

It should not be difficult for us to justify spending on infrastructure. We need to collect and evaluate data, brand and market ourselves, fundraise, set up financial systems, and recruit and retain top talent.

Right now, we're lying to everyone—our funders ("Our overhead is under 15 percent"), our individual donors ("100 percent of your donation will go to programs"), and even the IRS ("We didn't spend anything on fundraising last year"). In the Nonprofit Overhead Cost Study of nonprofit Form 990s, researchers found that more than a third reported no fundraising costs, while one in eight reported no management and general expenses (Gregory and Howard, 2009).

In fairness, the IRS's instructions are absurdly fuzzy. For example, the IRS does not define how to account for nonprofit marketing and communications.

We can, and should, earnestly consider our infrastructure needs, as well as the risks of underinvesting in these needs. Doing so may help us to focus on how infrastructure investments will benefit the people and communities for whom we are solving problems.

Once we're honest about what we need, we need to also understand what it really costs. We can also commit to being more truthful with our funders, our donors, and even the IRS. If more of us were honest with our funders, they would develop a more accurate picture of nonprofit overhead costs.

THE WAY FORWARD FOR THE NONPROFIT SECTOR
Gregory and Howard caution us that, "Changing funders' expectations… will require a coordinated, sector-wide effort." As a sector, we all must stand shoulder to shoulder.

We must push foundations to fund:

- The right causes: Invest a greater proportion of money to better help BIPOC and other marginalized communities. We know that currently the vast majority of funding helps a slight majority of the population.
- The root causes: Stop funding us based on siloed themes like health and education. "Every complex social problem has its roots everywhere, the environment, urban design, schools, diet, access to transport, as well as historical and cultural factors," wrote Villanueva. Also, stop focusing on increasing the number of people we help (downstream) instead of improving how much we help them (upstream).
- Advocacy: Fund our power. There's plenty more we can do besides lobbying to push the public agenda. It's not prohibited, and it's often necessary for massive systems change.
- The long game: Give us more time. Real change takes time, and support must be over long enough periods to show true impact. Foundations literally have all the time in the world.
- Leadership: Give us more than the measly 1 percent you currently give for leadership development. A percentage for leadership development should be added to every grant. Fund leadership development on collaboration skills. Reward organizations with a track record of

collaboration or those with a deep leadership bench over a single flashy leader.

- Collaboration: Fund us to collaborate in meaningful ways (including more integrated forms of collaboration) and with whom we know we need to combine forces. Broker connections to potential partners in non-binding ways.

We must also demand the following changes to foundation grant making structure:

- More general support: Commit a higher percentage of grant money for general operating grants. Even amidst the crises of 2020 and beyond, foundations continued to favor project grants; the number of general operating grants only increased by 3.5 percent. General operating grants accounted for 46.3 percent of all 2020 grants, while project-specific grants accounted for 53.7 percent (Foundation Source 2021). Do more.
- Cover overhead: Pay a greater and more accurate share of indirect costs on project-specific grants. Alternatively, allow grantees to define their true costs in grant applications and then cover those costs. (The board of Independent Sector believes in this approach so strongly that it issued a statement in 2004 encouraging funders to pay "the fair proportion of administrative and fundraising costs necessary to manage and sustain whatever is required by the organization to run that particular project" [Gregory and Howard, 2009].)
- Lighten up: Scale back your burdensome requirements in your applications, reports, and evaluations so that we can spend more of our valuable time actually doing the work. Since the beginning of COVID-19, more than 780

foundations pledged to give grantees flexibility in using grant money (Buteau et al, 2020). In a July 2020 survey, more than 85 percent of respondents were adopting flexible grantmaking practices for existing grantees such as loosened restrictions, reduced reporting requirements, and extended timelines (COF 2020). Make these changes permanent.

- Improve access: Open your grant opportunities to more nonprofit organizations and take away your restrictions on unsolicited proposals. Stop redlining organizations led by people of the communities we are all, collectively, trying to help.

Lastly, we must challenge foundations to improve their:

- Representation: Address your overwhelmingly white cultures and get better at representation from having engaged the groups you seek to help.

Villanueva warns us that representation is not the whole solution. "The issue is not recruitment of diverse humans—the 'pipeline' focus of the past, laying a seat at the table, as is often said—the issue is creating a culture of respect, curiosity, acceptance, and love. It's about fundamentally changing organizational culture, what constitutes acceptable behavior, and the definitions of success and leadership. It's about building ourselves a whole new table—one where we truly belong." Many diversity, equity, and inclusion experts are shifting our sector's thinking from "culture fit" to "culture add."

- Asset distribution: Increase the minimum distribution requirement—and eliminate staff and administrative fees—to add billions to the nonprofit sector's collective coffers. Each 1 percent increase in the required distribution would result in an additional $11 to $12.6 billion for nonprofits annually (Charity Stimulus 2022).

- Transparency: Share outcomes and results so we all might learn from them. "We should expect an assessment of whether all the billions of dollars foundations and other donors have poured into our communities have enabled nonprofits to solve the nation's most serious and recalcitrant issues and problems," wrote Eisenberg. Also be transparent around where your assets are invested. Ideally, your investments should be aligned with your mission.

OUR COLLECTIVE POWER

So how will we make this happen?

Together we will spark healthy debate and deliver constructive criticism. When an army of respected nonprofit leaders push back against antiquated grant making practices, foundations will need to adapt. As painful and scary as it might be, we will vote with our feet and walk away when a foundation doesn't support what we are trying to accomplish.

We will appeal to associations of foundations and other organizations dedicated to improving philanthropic effectiveness to push change within their ranks and set examples for the rest of the field.

If foundations do not adjust based on this pressure, we will advocate to change policies and laws that shield foundations' transparency and accountability. We will appeal to Congress—like Eisenberg did in 2004—about the power dynamics between foundations and organizations that serve the public good. We will lobby to increase the minimum foundation asset distribution and to exclude administrative costs from those distributions.

If it comes to it, we know how to organize. We know how public outrage can apply pressure on institutions. As a sector, we can bring foundations with opaque, inequitable, and burdensome practices to the court of public opinion.

Onward to Solving Instead of Serving

Our current societal problems are too big for us to be satisfied with having mediocre impacts through timid, incremental missions and programs. Our sector has the talent, the tools, and the passion to drive real social change; we just need a few boosts.

We need to focus on what really matters, pushing as far upstream as we can with laser focus and disciplined strategy. When the community needs feel so overwhelming, it can be hard to take the time and mental space to think about these things. (Trust me, I prod people to think about long-term strategy for a living.) However, a little long-term thinking and planning can dramatically transform our organizations' capacity for impact.

We need to build sustainable leadership to carry today's experience and lessons through to tomorrow. Our leaders are every bit as deserving of development as any other sector's, and it's time we put a stake in the ground. We have huge opportunities to invite previously excluded voices into the conversations about solutions. We also must continue to watch out for the next important trends that will influence our work.

We need to, in the words of Eisenberg, "inject a dose of courage into our individual and collective spines." We must confidently seek the rewards of testing hypotheses, trying new things, and collaborating in new ways. The very next thing somebody—or a coalition of somebodies—tries in the pursuit of solving a huge societal problem could be the answer.

We need to fight through our aversion and learn some important tricks from the for-profit sector. It will serve our missions well to treat ourselves, our colleagues, and subsequently our work with the respect it deserves. We can use our creativity and ability to connect emotionally and compete for everyone's eight seconds of attention and embrace big data as a friend.

Lastly, we need to push back against literally centuries of opaque, inequitable, and burdensome foundation funding. We must demand the space and grace to do our best work for the needs and communities we know so well. Our individual and collective efforts can shift these unhelpful funding practices so we can get what we need to truly solve our massive societal problems.

I have faith that, together, we can turn that faucet handle. Are you with me?

Acknowledgments

Writing this book was a wild ride, and both more challenging and more rewarding than I ever could have imagined. That's my name on the cover, but I could not have done this without the support, skills, encouragement, and extreme patience of a flotilla of great people.

Thank you to the wise and wonderful professionals who were willing to share their expertise and experiences with the non-profit and philanthropic sectors:

Adam Fong, Adam Tenner, Amse Heck, Anna Prow, Bill Novelli, Bill Skach, Billy Shore, Carla Ganiel, Dan Cardinali, Erica Parker, Heather Peeler, James Siegal, John Kern, John Kim, John Vranas, Kathy Bremer, Katrina VanHuss, Katya Andreson, Louise Buchanan, Meg Booth, Megan Schuknecht, Nick Richard, Roopal Saran, Rosemary Shahan, Sally Sachar, Saunji Fyffe, and Wendy Jackson.

Thank you to the talented and patient beta readers who helped me turn lumpy pieces of clay into something recognizable:

Susan Flinn, Anna Prow, Natalie Grandison, Ashley Ridlon, Christina Herold, Heather Robinson, Carla Ganiel, Darcey Mamone, Joan DeFilippo, Jane Repensek, and Warren Weissman.

Thank you to the most amazing team of friends, family, and champions of the nonprofit sector who provided the financial support that made this book possible:

Adam Tenner

Allison Gilmore

Alyssa Clark

Amanda Hazelwood

Andrea Lurie

Anna Prow

Annemarie Spadafore

Ashley Ridlon

Becky Miller

Bill Griffin

Billy Shore

Brian Thibeau

Briana Thibeau

Cady North

Caitlin Glasscock

Carla Ganiel

Carrie Tiller

Cary Gibson

Chris Urquiaga

Christina Carro

Christoph Haugstetter

Darcey Mamone

Deborah Smith

Deborah Wolfe

Dennis Gibson

Doug Foote

Eddie Rivas

Elizabeth Eastwick

Elizabeth Fallon

Eric Koester

Heather Peeler

Janey Repensek

Jeff Haslow

Jennifer Dumas

Jessica Ault

Joan DeFilippo

Jud Richland

Karen Dowling

Karen Griffin

Kate Cuffari

Katharine Brewer

Kathleen Unroe

Kathryn Sacco Jensen

Katie Ravenwood

Katrina VanHuss

Katya Andresen

Kevin Griffin

Kristin Neilson

LeighAnne Markaity

Lisa Hazelwood

Meg Booth

Meghan Powers

Michael Guerrino

Morgan St. Maxens

Natalie Watson

Nathan Armstrong

Nicole Friend

Rachel Gendreau

Rebecca Brown

Rebecca Katz

Richard Khoe

Roopal Saran

Sammy Dweck

Shay Thomson

Stephanie Baldwin

Susan Flinn

Ward Breeze

Thank you to Jessica Ault for contributing her librarian magic to the Appendix.

Thank you to Annemarie Spadafore, who is not only a stellar human being and loyal friend, but also the "sophomore" to my "freshman" in our author program. She is an inspiration!

A massive thank you to Caitlyn Conville of New Degree Press for her insightful and incisive editing. She pushed me to make this a much better book. A special thank you to Eric Koester—his support and superb motivational skills truly made this challenging process so enjoyable.

Last but not least, thank you to the nonprofit sector. It may be far from perfect, but it has my heart, and I fully believe it will be the sector to solve our biggest societal problems. Those of us who continue to give our time, talent, and treasure here will indeed make the world a better place.

Appendix

INTRODUCTION

Cowen, Tyler. "It's Not the Inequality; It's the Immobility." *The New York Times*, April 3, 2015, sec. The Upshot. https://www.nytimes.com/2015/04/05/upshot/its-not-the-inequality-its-the-immobility.html.

"The Human Needs Index (HNI) | The Salvation Army." n.d. Human Needs Index. Accessed February 21, 2022. https://humanneedsindex.org/.

Independent Sector. *The Charitable Sector.* Accessed January 4, 2022. https://independentsector.org/about/the-charitable-sector/

Le, Vu. 2016. "Dear Business People, Please Stop Bizsplaining Things to Us Nonprofit Folks." *Nonprofit AF* (blog). March 21, 2016. https://nonprofitaf.com/2016/03/dear-business-people-please-stop-bizsplaining-things-to-us-nonprofit-folks/.

World Health Organization. *Mental Health.* Accessed January 22, 2022. https://www.who.int/westernpacific/health-topics/ mental-health.

"The Nonprofit Sector in Brief." National Center for Charitable Statistics. June 18, 2020. https://nccs.urban.org/project/non-profit-sector-brief.

Pew Research Center. "Results First Clearinghouse Database." Data Visualization. Updated December 6, 2021. https://www. pewtrusts.org/en/research-and-analysis/data-visualiza-tions/2015/results-first-clearinghouse-database.

Salamon, Lester and Chelsea L. Newhouse. "2020 Nonprofit Employment Report." Johns Hopkins Center for Civil Society Studies. Nonprofit Economic Data Bulletin no. 48. June 2020.

"Structural Racism in America." Urban Institute. April 20, 2020. https://www.urban.org/features/structural-racism-america.

"Tracking the COVID-19 Economy's Effects on Food, Housing, and Employment Hardships." Center on Budget and Policy Priorities. November 10, 2021. https://www.cbpp.org/research/ poverty-and-inequality/tracking-the-covid-19-economys-ef-fects-on-food-housing-and.

United States Census Bureau. "Income and Poverty in the United States: 2020." Census.Gov. September 14, 2021. https://www. census.gov/library/publications/2021/demo/p60-273.html.

CHAPTER 1.1

Arnsberger, Paul, Melissa Ludlum, Margaret Riley, and Mark Stanton. "A History of the Tax-Exempt Sector: An SOI Perspective." *Statistics of Income Bulletin* (2008): 105–135.

Faulk, Lewis, Mirae Kim, Teresa Derrick-Mills, Elizabeth T. Boris, Laura Tomasko, Nora Hakizimana, Tianyu Chen, Minjung Kim, and Layla Nath. "Nonprofit Trends and Impacts 2021." Urban Institute. October 6, 2021. https://www.urban.org/research/publication/nonprofit-trends-and-impacts-2021.

Hammack, David C. "Introduction: Growth, Transformation, and Quiet Revolution in the Nonprofit Sector Over Two Centuries." *Nonprofit and Voluntary Sector Quarterly* 30 no. 2 (2001): 157–73. https://doi.org/10.1177/0899764001302001.

Hammack, David C. "Nonprofit Organizations in American History: Research Opportunities and Sources." *American Behavioral Psychologist* 45 no. 11 (2002): 1638–74.

Independent Sector. *The Charitable Sector.* Accessed January 4, 2022. https://independentsector.org/about/the-charitable-sector/

Internal Revenue Service. "Exemption Requirements - 501(c)(3) Organizations." Churches and Religious Organizations. Accessed January 6, 2022. https://www.irs.gov/charities-non-profits/charitable-organizations/exemption-requirements-501c3-organizations.

Meehan, III, William, Kim Starkey Jonker, and Jim Collins. *Engine of Impact: Essentials of Strategic Leadership in the Nonprofit*

Sector. 1st edition. Redwood City: Stanford Business Books, 2009.

"The Nonprofit Sector in Brief." National Center for Charitable Statistics. June 18, 2020. https://nccs.urban.org/project/nonprofit-sector-brief.

"Reviewing the History of Philanthropy in Black Education." *Diverse: Issues In Higher Education*. February 2, 2000. https://www.diverseeducation.com/home/article/15076763/reviewing-the-history-of-philanthropy-in-black-education.

Salamon, Lester and Chelsea L. Newhouse. "2020 Nonprofit Employment Report." Johns Hopkins Center for Civil Society Studies. Nonprofit Economic Data Bulletin no. 48. June 2020.

"State of the Nonprofit Sector Survey." NFF. 2018 Survey Results. 2018. https://nff.org/sites/default/files/paragraphs/file/download/PackardFinalCombine.2.pdf

CHAPTER 1.2

Agrawal, Shantanu, and Adaeze Enekwechi. "It's Time To Address The Role Of Implicit Bias Within Health Care Delivery." *Health Affairs*. January 15, 2020. https://www.healthaffairs.org/do/10.1377/forefront.20200108.34515/full/.

American Civil Liberties Union. "Systemic Equality: Addressing America's Legacy of Racism and Systemic Discrimination" Churches and Religious Organizations." News. Last updated on October 15, 2021. https://www.aclu.org/news/topic/system-

ic-equality-addressing-americas-legacy-of-racism-and-system-
ic-discrimination/

Desjardins, Jeff. "How Long Does It Take to Hit 50 Million Users?"
Visual Capitalist. June 8, 2018. https://www.visualcapitalist.
com/how-long-does-it-take-to-hit-50-million-users/.

Meehan, III, William, Kim Starkey Jonker, and Jim Collins. *Engine
of Impact: Essentials of Strategic Leadership in the Nonprofit
Sector*. 1st edition. Redwood City: Stanford Business Books,
2019.

Pestana, Jose V., and Nuria Codina. "Being Conscious of One's
Own Heroism: An Empirical Approach to Analyzing the Lead-
ership Potential of Future CEOs." *Frontiers in Psychology* 9
(January 2019): 2787. https://doi.org/10.3389/fpsyg.2018.02787.

Silver, Nate. "There Are Few Libertarians. But Many Americans
Have Libertarian Views." *FiveThirtyEight* (blog). April 9, 2015.
https://fivethirtyeight.com/features/there-are-few-libertari-
ans-but-many-americans-have-libertarian-views/.

Sustainable Economies Law Center. "Worker Self-Directed Nonprofits." Cooperative Resources and Projects. Accessed January
11, 2022. https://www.theselc.org/worker_selfdirected_non-
profits.

CHAPTER 2.1

Centers for Disease Control and Prevention. "Child Health." Last
reviewed: February 1, 2022. https://www.cdc.gov/nchs/fastats/
child-health.htm.

Heath, Dan. *Upstream: The Quest to Solve Problems Before They Happen*. Illustrated edition. New York: Avid Reader Press / Simon & Schuster, 2020.

Hindery, Robin. "Researchers Explore Role of Culture in Decision to Get a Mammogram." *University of California San Francisco*. September 2, 2009. https://www.ucsf.edu/news/2009/09/103289/researchers-explore-role-culture-decision-get-mammogram.

CHAPTER 2.2

Meehan, III, William, Kim Starkey Jonker, and Jim Collins. *Engine of Impact: Essentials of Strategic Leadership in the Nonprofit Sector*. 1st edition. Redwood City: Stanford Business Books, 2019.

Reid, Margaret F., Lynne Brown, Denise McNerney, and Dominic J. Perri. "Time to Raise the Bar on Nonprofit Strategic Planning and Implementation." *Strategy & Leadership* 42 no.3 (2014): 31–39. https://doi.org/10.1108/SL-03-2014-0019.

Sargeant, Adrian, and Harriet Day. "Wake-Up Call: A Study of Nonprofit Leadership in the US." *Boardable (blog)*. August 29, 2018. https://boardable.com/blog/study-of-nonprofit-leadership/.

CHAPTER 2.3

Heath, Dan. *Upstream: The Quest to Solve Problems Before They Happen*. Illustrated edition. New York: Avid Reader Press / Simon & Schuster, 2020.

Meehan, III, William, Kim Starkey Jonker, and Jim Collins. *Engine of Impact: Essentials of Strategic Leadership in the Nonprofit Sector*. 1st edition. Redwood City: Stanford Business Books, 2019.

Reid, Margaret F., Lynne Brown, Denise McNerney, and Dominic J. Perri. "Time to Raise the Bar on Nonprofit Strategic Planning and Implementation." *Strategy & Leadership* 42 no.3 (2014): 31–39. https://doi.org/10.1108/SL-03-2014-0019.

Sargeant, Adrian, and Harriet Day. "Wake-Up Call: A Study of Nonprofit Leadership in the US." *Boardable (blog)*. August 29, 2018. https://boardable.com/blog/study-of-nonprofit-leadership/.

CHAPTER 3.1

Allison, Scott T., and George R. Goethals. "'Now He Belongs to the Ages': The Heroic Leadership Dynamic and Deep Narratives of Greatness." *Conceptions of Leadership: Enduring Ideas and Emerging Insights*, edited by George R. Goethals, Scott T. Allison, Roderick M. Kramer, and David M. Messick, 167–83. New York: Palgrave Macmillan, 2014.

Allison, Scott T., and George R. Goethals. "How Hero Stories Energize Us." (blog) January 28, 2015. https://blog.richmond.edu/heroes/2015/01/28/the-heroic-leadership-dynamic-part-3-how-hero-stories-energize-us/

Ashoka. *Ashoka's History*. Accessed December 13, 2021. https://www.ashoka.org/en-us/story/ashokas-history

Bennis, Warren. "The Challenges of Leadership in the Modern World: Introduction to the Special Issue." *American Psychologist* 62 no. 1 (2007): 2–5. https://doi.org/10.1037/0003-066X.62.1.2.

Callanan, Laura, Lenny Mendonca, and Doug Scott. "What Social-Sector Leaders Need to Succeed." McKinsey & Co. November 1, 2014. https://www.mckinsey.com/industries/public-and-social-sector/our-insights/what-social-sector-leaders-need-to-succeed.

Callanan, Laura, Nora Silver, and Paul Jansen. "Leveraging Social Sector Leadership." Grantmakers for Effective Organizations, Haas School of Business, University of California, Berkeley. 2015. https://haas.berkeley.edu/wp-content/uploads/GEO_2015_leveraging_leadership.pdf.

Crutchfield, Leslie R. *How Change Happens: Why Some Social Movements Succeed While Others Don't.* 1st edition. Hoboken: Wiley, 2018.

"New Bridgespan Study of 15 of the Greatest Social Impact Stories of the 20th Century Reveals How Philanthropy Can Advance Large-Scale Systems Change." Bridgespan Group. August 22, 2017. https://www.bridgespan.org/about-us/for-the-media/new-bridgespan-study-of-15-of-the-greatest-social.

Riggio, Ronald, and Heidi Riggio. "Social Psychology and Charismatic Leadership." *Leadership at the Crossroads: Social Psychology and Leadership,* (2008) 30–44.

Schein, Seth L. *The Mortal Hero: An Introduction to Homer's Iliad.* Berkeley: University of California Press, 1984.

Shaw, David. "Hunger for Heroes, Villains Rooted in American Psyche : Media: In a Society That Venerates the Individual over Community, Coverage Often Glorifies Fame—and Infamy." *Los Angeles Times.* February 17, 1994. https://www.latimes.com/archives/la-xpm-1994-02-17-mn-24090-story.html.

CHAPTER 3.2

Bennis, Warren. "The Challenges of Leadership in the Modern World: Introduction to the Special Issue." *American Psychologist* 62 no. 1 (2007): 2–5. https://doi.org/10.1037/0003-066X.62.1.2.

Crutchfield, Leslie R. *How Change Happens: Why Some Social Movements Succeed While Others Don't.* 1st edition. Hoboken: Wiley, 2018.

Fernandez, Idalia, and Allison Brown. "The State of Diversity in the Nonprofit Sector." *Community Wealth Partners,* May 12, 2015. https://communitywealth.com/the-state-of-diversity-in-the-nonprofit-sector/.

Herway, Jake. "How to Create a Culture of Psychological Safety." *Gallup.* December 7, 2017. https://www.gallup.com/workplace/236198/create-culture-psychological-safety.aspx.

McCoy, Jonathan, and Becky Endicott. "Real Talk: Why Nonprofits Must Dream Bigger - Dan Pallotta." May 10, 2021. In *We*

Are For Good. Podcast, MP3 audio, 47.08. https://www.weare-forgood.com/episode/115.

The Annie E. Casey Foundation. 2008. "Ready to Lead?" The Annie E. Casey Foundation. January 1, 2008. https://www.aecf.org/resources/ready-to-lead.

Rock, David, and Heidi Grant. "Why Diverse Teams Are Smarter." *Harvard Business Review,* November 4, 2016. https://hbr.org/2016/11/why-diverse-teams-are-smarter.

Sinek, Simon. "How Great Leaders Inspire Action." Filmed September 2009 at TEDxPuget Sound, Newcastle, WA. Video, 17:48. https://www.ted.com/talks/simon_sinek_how_great_leaders_inspire_action.

Torres, Roselinde. "What It Takes to Be a Great Leader." Filmed October 2013 at TED@BCG, San Francisco, CA. Video, 9:07. https://www.ted.com/talks/roselinde_torres_what_it_takes_to_be_a_great_leader?language=en.

"UsAgainstAlzheimer's Applauds Progress with New Lilly and Eisai/Biogen Drug Treatments That Offer the Promise of More Choices to Alzheimer's Patients." UsAgainstAlzheimer's. June 24, 2021. https://www.usagainstalzheimers.org/press/usagainstalzheimers-applauds-progress-new-lilly-and-eisa-ibiogen-drug-treatments-offer-promise

Weiner, Yitzi. "Social Impact Heroes: Why & How George Vradenburg of UsAgainstAlzheimer's Is Helping To Change Our World." *Authority Magazine* (blog). April 8, 2021. https://medium.com/authority-magazine/social-impact-heroes-why-how-george-vradenburg-of-usagainstalzheimers-is-helping-to-change-our-7ba6b063ad88.

"What Is Psychological Safety at Work?" Center for Creative Leadership. January 15, 2022. https://www.ccl.org/articles/leading-effectively-articles/what-is-psychological-safety-at-work/

CHAPTER 3.3

2021 Annual Report: State of the Nonprofit Sector. Springfield, MO: BKD, 2021. https://www.bkd.com/media/state-nonprofit-sector-report-2021.

"The 70-20-10 Rule for Leadership Development." Center for Creative Leadership. November 24, 2020. https://www.ccl.org/articles/leading-effectively-articles/70-20-10-rule/.

Alcoholics Anonymous. *What is AA?* Accessed January 15, 2022. https://www.aa.org/what-is-aa

Brafman, Ori, and Rod A. Beckstrom. *The Starfish and the Spider: The Unstoppable Power of Leaderless Organizations.* Reprint edition. London: Portfolio, 2008.

Brew, Atokatha Ashmond. "2021 Nonprofit Talent Retention Survey Results." Nonprofit HR. September 23, 2021. https://www.nonprofithr.com/2021talentretentionsurvey/.

Callanan, Laura, Lenny Mendonca, and Doug Scott. "What Social-Sector Leaders Need to Succeed." McKinsey & Co. November 1, 2014. https://www.mckinsey.com/industries/public-and-social-sector/our-insights/what-social-sector-leaders-need-to-succeed.

Callanan, Laura, Nora Silver, and Paul Jansen. "Leveraging Social Sector Leadership." Grantmakers for Effective Organizations, Haas School of Business, University of California, Berkeley. 2015. https://haas.berkeley.edu/wp-content/uploads/GEO_2015_leveraging_leadership.pdf.

Linnell, Deborah, and Tim Wolfred. 2010. "Creative Disruption: Sabbaticals For Capacity Building And Leadership Development." NCFP. January 23, 2010. https://www.ncfp.org/knowledge/creative-disruption-sabbaticals-for-capacity-building-and-leadership-development-in-the-nonprofit-sector/.

Meehan, III, William, Kim Starkey Jonker, and Jim Collins. *Engine of Impact: Essentials of Strategic Leadership in the Nonprofit Sector*. 1st edition. Redwood City: Stanford Business Books, 2019.

Sargeant, Adrian, and Harriet Day. "Wake-Up Call: A Study of Nonprofit Leadership in the US." Boardable. 2018. https://boardable.com/blog/study-of-nonprofit-leadership/.

Smith, Mistinguette. "Nonprofit Leadership at a Crossroads." *Nonprofit Quarterly*. September 17, 2019. https://nonprofitquarterly.org/nonprofit-leadership-at-a-crossroads/.

Trellis Partners. *Term Executive Services*. Accessed December 10, 2021. https://trellispartners.org/services/

PART 4 INTRODUCTION

Merriam-Webster. s.v. "bravery (n.)." Accessed January 25, 2022.
   https://www.merriam-webster.com/dictionary/bravery

CHAPTER 4.1

Cystic Fibrosis Foundation. "Our History." About Us. Accessed
   November 14, 2021. https://www.cff.org/about-us/our-history

Utley, Tori. "Why Nonprofit Organizations Should Take Risks
   More Often — Even If It Means Failure." *Forbes.* October 28,
   2016. https://www.forbes.com/sites/toriutley/2016/10/28/why-
   nonprofit-organizations-should-take-risks-more-often-even-
   if-it-means-failure/.

CHAPTER 4.2

2021 Annual Report: State of the Nonprofit Sector. Springfield, MO:
   BKD, 2021. https://www.bkd.com/media/state-nonprofit-sec-
   tor-report-2021.

Atwell, Mattew, John Bridgeland, Eleanor Manspile, Bob Balfanz,
   and Vaughan Byrnes. Building A Grad Nation. Produced by
   Civic, the Everyone Graduates Center at the Johns Hopkins
   University School of Education, America's Promise Alliance
   and the Alliance for Excellent Education. October 6, 2021.
   http://americaspromise.org//report/2021-building-grad-na-
   tion-report.

Chambers, Sam. "War on Smoking." *BloombergQuint.* Last
   Updated December 17, 2017. https://www.bloombergquint.com/
   quicktakes/war-smoking.

Crutchfield, Leslie R. *How Change Happens: Why Some Social Movements Succeed While Others Don't.* 1st edition. Hoboken: Wiley, 2018.

"Is It Time to Close?" AIDS United. December 2015. https://aidsunited.org/is-it-time-to-close/.

McCammon, Ross. "What Makes a Perfect Collaboration? Weakness, Conflict and Doughnuts." *Entrepreneur.* June 22, 2012. https://www.entrepreneur.com/article/223624.

McKeon, Albert. "The Fear of Uncertainty Can Be a Genuine Struggle." *Now. Powered by Northrop Grumman* (blog). January 15, 2021. https://now.northropgrumman.com/the-fear-of-uncertainty-can-be-a-genuine-struggle/.

Novelli, Bill. *Good Business: The Talk, Fight, Win Way to Change the World.* Baltimore: Johns Hopkins University Press, 2021.

CHAPTER 4.3

Case, Jean. *Be Fearless: 5 Principles for a Life of Breakthroughs and Purpose.* New York: Simon & Schuster, 2019.

Barden, Pamela. "Why Are Nonprofits Afraid to Take Risks When It Comes to Fundraising?" *NonProfit PRO.* October 12, 2010. https://www.nonprofitpro.com/post/why-nonprofits-afraid-take-risks-comes-fundraising/.

Brenner, Laila, and Darian Rodriguez Heyman. *Nonprofit Management 101: A Complete and Practical Guide for Leaders and Professionals.* 2nd edition. Hoboken, Wiley, 2019.

Brown, Brené. *Rising Strong: How the Ability to Reset Transforms the Way We Live, Love, Parent, and Lead*. New York: Random House, 2017.

Fail Forward. *Intelligent Failure*. Accessed January 10, 2022. https://failforward.org/intelligent-failure#what-is-intelligent-failure

Gino, Francesca, and Bradley Staats. "Why Organizations Don't Learn." *Harvard Business Review*, November 1, 2015. https://hbr.org/2015/11/why-organizations-dont-learn.

Jensen, Christopher. "50 Years Ago, 'Unsafe at Any Speed' Shook the Auto World." *The New York Times*, November 26, 2015. https://www.nytimes.com/2015/11/27/automobiles/50-years-ago-unsafe-at-any-speed-shook-the-auto-world.html.

Peacock Rebellion. *About Us*. Accessed February 22, 2022. https://peacockrebellion.org/about

Rare. *Green Benefits*. Accessed December 20, 2021. https://rare.org/green-benefits/

Shiv, Baba. "Baba Shiv: Why Failure Drives Innovation." Stanford Graduate School of Business (blog). March 1, 2011. https://www.gsb.stanford.edu/insights/baba-shiv-why-failure-drives-innovation.

CHAPTER 5.1

"6 Pitfalls of Lack of Accountability in the Workplace." Culture Partners (blog). Accessed February 12, 2022. https://culture.io/pitfalls-of-lack-workplace-accountability/.

"Are Low Performers Destroying Your Culture and Driving Away Your Best Employees? Here's What You Can Do." Eagle Hill National Attrition Survey, Eagle Hill Consulting. 2015. https://www.eaglehillconsulting.com/wp-content/uploads/ Eagle-Hill-Consulting_Attrition-White-Paper.pdf.

Drucker, Peter. "Work and Tools." *Technology and Culture* 1, no. 1 (Winter 1959): 28-37. https://www.jstor.org/stable/3100785?-origin=crossref.

Herrera, Tim. "Your Workplace Isn't Your Family (and That's O.K.!)." *The New York Times*, August 13, 2018. https://www. nytimes.com/2018/08/13/smarter-living/your-workplace-isnt-your-family-and-thats-ok.html.

Ryan, Liz. "The Ugly Truth About Team-Building." *Forbes*. September 22, 2016. https://www.forbes.com/sites/lizryan/2016/09/22/ the-ugly-truth-about-team-building/.

Yohn, Denise Lee. "Stop Saying Your Company Is Like A Family." *Forbes*. November 5, 2019. https://www.forbes.com/sites/ deniselyohn/2019/11/05/stop-saying-your-company-is-like-a-family/.

CHAPTER 5.2

Anthony, James. "257 Marketing Statistics You Must See: 2021 Data Analysis & Market Share." *FinancesOnline*. November 18, 2019. https://financesonline.com/marketing-statistics/.

Arons, Marc de Swaan, Frank van den Driest, and Keith Weed. "The Ultimate Marketing Machine." *Harvard Business Review*,

July 1, 2014. https://hbr.org/2014/07/the-ultimate-marketing-machine.

"Attention Spans." Consumer Insights. Microsoft Canada. 2015 https://dl.motamem.org/microsoft-attention-spans-research-report.pdf.

Brenner, Laila, and Darian Rodriguez Heyman. *Nonprofit Management 101: A Complete and Practical Guide for Leaders and Professionals.* 2nd edition. Hoboken, Wiley, 2019.

Farhi, Paul. "National Geographic Gives Fox Control of Media Assets in $725 Million Deal." *Washington Post*, September 9, 2015, sec. Style. https://www.washingtonpost.com/lifestyle/style/national-geographic-magazine-shifts-to-for-profit-status-with-fox-partnership/2015/09/09/7c9f034e-56f0-11e5-8bb1-b488d231bba2_story.html.

Moorman, Christine. "Marketing Budgets Vary by Industry." *The Wall Street Journal.* January 24, 2017. https://deloitte.wsj.com/articles/who-has-the-biggest-marketing-budgets-1485234137.

Ramaswamy, Sridhar. "How Micro-Moments Are Changing the Rules." Think with Google. April 2015. https://www.thinkwithgoogle.com/marketing-strategies/app-and-mobile/how-micro-moments-are-changing-rules/.

Social Experience Forum. "Peter Economides | Social Experience Forum 2017." September 18, 2017. Video, 41:59. https://www.youtube.com/watch?v=6tGoMthQfiw&t=5s

CHAPTER 5.3

"2021 Harris Poll EquiTrend® Study." The Harris Poll. Accessed December 15, 2021. https://theharrispoll.com/equitrend/

"Are Low Performers Destroying Your Culture and Driving Away Your Best Employees? Here's What You Can Do." Eagle Hill National Attrition Survey, Eagle Hill Consulting. 2015. https://www.eaglehillconsulting.com/wp-content/uploads/ Eagle-Hill-Consulting_Attrition-White-Paper.pdf.

Arons, Marc de Swaan, Frank van den Driest, and Keith Weed. "The Ultimate Marketing Machine." *Harvard Business Review*, July 1, 2014. https://hbr.org/2014/07/the-ultimate-marketing-machine.

Pennington, Randy. "Building a Culture of Accountability." *HR Magazine*. September 1, 2015. https://www.shrm.org/hr-today/ news/hr-magazine/pages/0915-building-an-accountable-culture.aspx.

Sinek, Simon. "How Great Leaders Inspire Action." Filmed September 2009 at TEDxPuget Sound, Newcastle, WA. Video, 17:48. https://www.ted.com/talks/simon_sinek_how_great_ leaders_inspire_action.

Social Experience Forum. "Peter Economides | Social Experience Forum 2017." September 18, 2017. Video, 41:59. https://www. youtube.com/watch?v=6tGoMthQfiw&t=5s

"The State of Data in the Nonprofit Sector." everyaction and nonprofit hub. 2018. https://cdn2.hubspot.net/hubfs/433841/The_ State_of_Data_in_The_Nonprofit_Sector.pdf.

PART 6 INTRODUCTION

Foundation Source. "2021 Report On Private Foundations—Grant-making". Fairfield, CT: Foundation Source. 2021. https://foundationsource.com/wp-content/uploads/2021/12/2021-Report-on-Private-Foundations-Grantmaking_FINAL_122021.pdf.

Gregory, Ann Goggins, and Don Howard. "The Nonprofit Starvation Cycle." *Stanford Social Innovation Review.* 2009. https://ssir.org/articles/entry/the_nonprofit_starvation_cycle.

Reich, Robert. "Philanthropy in the Service of Democracy." *Stanford Social Innovation Review.* 2019. https://ssir.org/articles/entry/philanthropy_in_the_service_of_democracy.

CHAPTER 6.1

Council on Foundations-Commonfund. "2020 Study of Investment of Endowments for Private and Community Foundations." 2021. https://cffiles.blob.core.windows.net/files/Commonfund_Institute/CCSF/2020_Council-on-Foundations-Commonfund-Study-of-Foundations-SECURED.pdf

Eisenberg, Pablo. "The Nonprofit Sector and the Will to Change." *New England Journal of Public Policy* 20 no. 1 (2004): https://scholarworks.umb.edu/nejpp/vol20/iss1/20.

Eisenberg, Pablo. "Don't Leave Nonprofits Out of Philanthropy History." *The Chronicle of Philanthropy.* February 2, 2017. https://www.philanthropy.com/article/dont-leave-nonprofits-out-of-philanthropy-history/.

Emergency Charity Stimulus. *Letter*. Accessed February 22, 2022. http://charitystimulus.org/

Field, Anne. "Mission Accomplished: How The Heron Foundation Went 'All In.'" *Forbes*. March 30, 2017. https://www.forbes.com/sites/annefield/2017/03/30/mission-accomplished-how-the-heron-foundation-went-all-in/.

Foundation Advocate. "Holdings Disclosure: Who Owns What? And Who Is Not Saying." Accessed February 22, 2022. https://www.foundationadvocate.com/holdings-disclosure/.

Foundation Source. "2021 Report On Private Foundations – Grantmaking". Fairfield, CT: Foundation Source. 2021. https://foundationsource.com/wp-content/uploads/2021/12/2021-Report-on-Private-Foundations-Grantmaking_FINAL_122021.pdf.

Foundation Source. "Small to Mid-Size Foundations Exceed Minimum Distribution Requirements by Large Margin." Foundation Source press release, June 29, 2010. Foundation Source website. https://foundationsource.com/resources/press-releases/small-to-mid-size-foundations-exceed-minimum-distribution-requirements-by-large-margin/

The Giving Practice. "Forging Ahead." Tools and Guides. November 21, 2018. https://philanthropynw.org/resources/forging-ahead.

"Giving USA 2021: In a Year of Unprecedented Events and Challenges, Charitable Giving Reached a Record $471.44 Billion in

2020." *Lilly Family School of Philanthropy*. June 15, 2021. https://
philanthropy.iupui.edu/news-events/news-item/index.html.

"Key Facts on U.S. Nonprofits and Foundations" https://candid.
issuelab.org/resource/key-facts-on-u-s-nonprofits-and-foun-
dations.html. April 2020.

Meehan, III, William, Kim Starkey Jonker, and Jim Collins. *Engine
of Impact: Essentials of Strategic Leadership in the Nonprofit
Sector*. 1st edition. Redwood City: Stanford Business Books,
2019.

Milway, Katie, and William Galligan. "The Myth of Perpetuity
in Foundation Strategy." *Stanford Social Innovation Review*,
December 11, 2020. https://ssir.org/articles/entry/the_myth_
of_perpetuity_in_foundation_strategy.

Reich, Robert. "What Are Foundations For?" *Boston Review*. May
28, 2013. https://bostonreview.net/forum/foundations-philan-
thropy-democracy/.

"Shifting Practices, Sharing Power? How U.S. Philanthropy Is
Responding to the 2020 Crises." Council on Foundations.
September 15, 2020. https://www.cof.org/content/shift-
ing-practices-sharing-power-how-us-philanthropy-respond-
ing-2020-crises.

Villanueva, Edgar. *Decolonizing Wealth: Indigenous Wisdom to
Heal Divides and Restore Balance*. Oakland: Berrett-Koehler
Publishers, 2018.

Villarosa, Lori. "Reports of a Massive Increase in Racial-Justice Funding Paint a Distorted and Dangerous Picture." *The Chronicle of Philanthropy*. September 21, 2021. https://www.philanthropy.com/article/reports-of-a-massive-increase-in-racial-justice-funding-paint-a-distorted-and-dangerous-picture.

CHAPTER 6.2

Bennett, Jackie, Cayla Damick, Kyle Layne, Ben Murphy, Daniel Salas, Ben Murphy, Kirsten Swanson, and Ali Webb. 2021. "Strategic Philanthropy Gets a Wake-Up Call." *Nonprofit Quarterly*. February 8, 2021. https://nonprofitquarterly.org/strategic-philanthropy-gets-a-wake-up-call/.

Biery, Mary Ellen. "A Sure-Fire Way To Boost The Bottom Line." *Forbes*. January 12, 2014. https://www.forbes.com/sites/sageworks/2014/01/12/control-overhead-compare-industry-data/.

brown, adrienne maree. *Emergent Strategy: Shaping Change, Changing Worlds*. Oakland: AK Press, 2014.

Buteau, Ellie, Satla Marotta, Hannah Martin, Naomi Orensten, and Kate Gehling. "New Attitudes, Old Practices: The Provision of Multiyear General Operating Support." *The Center for Effective Philanthropy* (blog). 2020. https://cep.org/portfolio/new-attitudes-old-practices/.

Callanan, Laura, Lenny Mendonca, and Doug Scott. "What Social-Sector Leaders Need to Succeed." *McKinsey & Co.* November 1, 2014. https://www.mckinsey.com/industries/public-and-social-sector/our-insights/what-social-sector-leaders-need-to-succeed.

"Criteria for Philanthropy at Its Best: Benchmarks to Assess and Enhance Grantmaker Impact." National Committee for Responsive Philanthropy. n.d. https://www.ncrp.org/about-us/philanthropy-at-its-best.

Daniels, Alex, and Dan Parks. 2020. "Nine in 10 Foundations Say They Provide Aid for Advocacy Efforts." *The Chronicle of Philanthropy.* May 13, 2020. https://www.philanthropy.com/article/nine-in-10-foundations-say-they-provide-aid-for-advocacy-efforts/.

Easterling, Douglas, and Laura McDuffee. "How Can Foundations Promote Impactful Collaboration?" *The Foundation Review* 11 no. 3 (2019). https://doi.org/10.9707/1944-5660.1479.

Eckhart-Queenan, Jeri, Michael Etzel, and Julia Silverman. "Five Foundations Address the 'Starvation Cycle.'" The Chronicle of Philanthropy. August 22, 2019

Foster, William, Gail Perreault, Alison Powell, and Chris Addy. "Making Big Bets for Social Change." Stanford Social Innovation Review 14, no. 1 (2015): 26–35. https://doi.org/10.48558/3SAH-R095.

Gregory, Ann Goggins, and Don Howard. "The Nonprofit Starvation Cycle." *Stanford Social Innovation Review.* 2009. https://ssir.org/articles/entry/the_nonprofit_starvation_cycle.

Guerriero, Patrick, and Susan Wolf Ditkoff. "When Philanthropy Meets Advocacy." *Stanford Social Innovation Review.* 2018. https://ssir.org/articles/entry/when_philanthropy_meets_advocacy.

Jones, Nicholas, Rachel Marks, Roberto Ramirez, Merarys Rios-Vargas. "2020 Census Illuminates Racial and Ethnic Composition of the Country." United States Census Bureau. August 12, 2021. https://www.census.gov/library/stories/2021/08/improved-race-ethnicity-measures-reveal-united-states-population-much-more-multiracial.html

Kania, John, Mark Kramer, and Patty Russell. "Strategic Philanthropy for a Complex World." *Stanford Social Innovation Review*. 2014. https://ssir.org/articles/entry/strategic_philanthropy.

Kasper, Gabriel, and Justin Marcoux. "The Re-Emerging Art of Funding Innovation." Stanford Social Innovation Review 12, no. 2 (2014): 28–35. https://ssir.org/articles/entry/the_re_emerging_art_of_funding_innovation

Laffitte, Helene. "History Of Consulting: The 8 Important Stages." *Consulting Quest*. May 31, 2019. https://consultingquest.com/insights/8-stages-history-of-consulting-2021/.

Neuhoff, Alex, Katie Smith Milway, Reilly Kiernan, and Josh Grehan. "Making Sense of Nonprofit Collaborations." The Bridgespan Group. December 2014.

"New Bridgespan Study of 15 of the Greatest Social Impact Stories of the 20th Century Reveals How Philanthropy Can Advance Large-Scale Systems Change." Bridgespan Group. August 22, 2017. https://www.bridgespan.org/about-us/for-the-media/new-bridgespan-study-of-15-of-the-greatest-social.

Pallota, Dan. "The Way We Think About Charity is Dead Wrong." Filmed February 2013 at TED2013, Long Beach, CA. Video, 18:38. https://www.ted.com/talks/dan_pallotta_the_way_we_think_about_charity_is_dead_wrong.

Reich, Robert. "Philanthropy in the Service of Democracy." *Stanford Social Innovation Review.* 2019. https://ssir.org/articles/entry/philanthropy_in_the_service_of_democracy.

"Shifting Practices, Sharing Power? How U.S. Philanthropy Is Responding to the 2020 Crises." Council on Foundations. September 15, 2020. https://www.cof.org/content/shifting-practices-sharing-power-how-us-philanthropy-responding-2020-crises.

Villanueva, Edgar. *Decolonizing Wealth: Indigenous Wisdom to Heal Divides and Restore Balance.* Oakland: Berrett-Koehler Publishers, 2018.

CHAPTER 6.3

Alexandria City Public Schools. "Brown v. Board and the Desegregation of ACPS." *History of ACPS.* Accessed February 15, 2022. https://www.acps.k12.va.us/Page/2402#:~:text=Board%20and%20the%20Desegregation%20of%20Alexandria%20City%20Public%20Schools,in%20public%20schools%20was%20unconstitutional.

The Annie E. Casey Foundation. "Virginia and The Annie E. Casey Foundation." *Where We Work.* Accessed January 25, 2022. https://www.aecf.org/where-we-work/location/va

The Kresge Foundation. "Detroit." *Our Work*. Accessed January 25, 2022. https://kresge.org/our-work/detroit/

CHAPTER 6.4

Buteau, Ellie, Satla Marotta, Hannah Martin, Naomi Orensten, and Kate Gehling. "New Attitudes, Old Practices: The Provision of Multiyear General Operating Support." *The Center for Effective Philanthropy (blog)*. 2020. https://cep.org/portfolio/new-attitudes-old-practices/.

Callanan, Laura, Lenny Mendonca, and Doug Scott. "What Social-Sector Leaders Need to Succeed." *McKinsey & Co.* November 1, 2014. https://www.mckinsey.com/industries/public-and-social-sector/our-insights/what-social-sector-leaders-need-to-succeed.

Council on Foundations. *Shifting Practices, Sharing Power? How U.S. Philanthropy Is Responding to the 2020 Crises*. September 15, 2020. https://www.cof.org/content/shifting-practices-sharing-power-how-us-philanthropy-responding-2020-crises.

Eisenberg, Pablo. "The Nonprofit Sector and the Will to Change." *New England Journal of Public Policy* 20 no. 1 (2004): https://scholarworks.umb.edu/nejpp/vol20/iss1/20.

Eisenberg, Pablo. "Don't Leave Nonprofits Out of Philanthropy History." *The Chronicle of Philanthropy*. February 2, 2017. https://www.philanthropy.com/article/dont-leave-nonprofits-out-of-philanthropy-history/.

Emergency Charity Stimulus. *Letter*. Accessed February 22, 2022. http://charitystimulus.org/

Foundation Source. "2021 Report On Private Foundations—Grantmaking". Fairfield, CT: Foundation Source. 2021. https://foundationsource.com/wp-content/uploads/2021/12/2021-Report-on-Private-Foundations-Grantmaking_FINAL_122021.pdf.

Gregory, Ann Goggins, and Don Howard. "The Nonprofit Starvation Cycle." *Stanford Social Innovation Review*. 2009. https://ssir.org/articles/entry/the_nonprofit_starvation_cycle.

Reich, Robert. "Philanthropy in the Service of Democracy." *Stanford Social Innovation Review*. 2019. https://ssir.org/articles/entry/philanthropy_in_the_service_of_democracy.

Villanueva, Edgar. *Decolonizing Wealth: Indigenous Wisdom to Heal Divides and Restore Balance*. Oakland: Berrett-Koehler Publishers, 2018.

CONCLUSION

Eisenberg, Pablo. "The Nonprofit Sector and the Will to Change." *New England Journal of Public Policy* 20 no. 1 (2004): https://scholarworks.umb.edu/nejpp/vol20/iss1/20.